Russian and Other Slavic Embroidery Designs

by Sandra Ley

Russian and Other Slavic Embroidery Designs
Fashion for Everyone: The Story of Ready-to-Wear
America's Sewing Book

Russian and Other Slavic Embroidery Designs

SANDRA LEY

Charles Scribner's Sons
New York

Drawings, charts, and diagrams by the author.
Photographs by Olga Ley.

Library of Congress Cataloging in Publication Data

Ley, Sandra.
Russian and other Slavic embroidery designs.

1. Embroidery—Patterns. 2. Design, Decorative—Russia. 3. Design, Decorative—Europe, Eastern. I. Title.
TT771.L49 746.4'4 76-12479
ISBN 0-684-14734-3

This book published simultaneously in the United States of America and in Canada—

1 3 5 7 9 11 13 15 17 19 MD/C 20 18 16 14 12 10 8 6 4 2

Printed in the United States of America

For my mother, Olga Ley

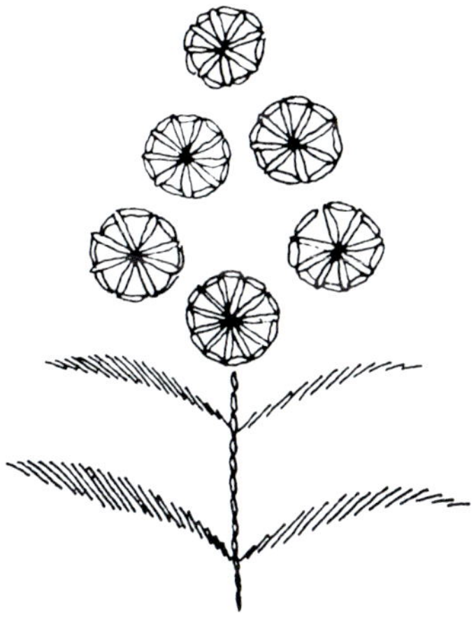

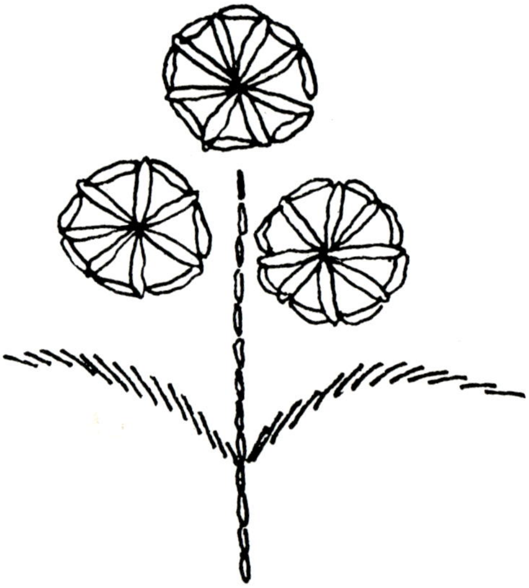

CONTENTS

Russian and Other Slavic Embroidery Designs

Introduction

The needlework of the Slavic peoples is one of the richest sources of design in the world. Embroidery, which was done mainly by peasant women, was used to decorate the national or "folk" costumes of the individual countries and regions, and for shirts, aprons, headgear, shawls, towels, tablecloths, curtains, and almost any other article made of fabric. The peasants of these countries, whose lives were spent in endless work and who were completely cut off from the rest of Europe, used embroidery to introduce an element of beauty into the monotony of their everyday lives. Because embroidery called for little in the way of tools—fabric, needles, and thread were all that were needed—it became perhaps the best developed of the folk arts.

Every historical period in the history of the Slavic peoples is reflected in the designs used for their needlework. The geometric symbols were first used in the primeval period; the epoch of Slavonic paganism introduced poetical mythology; heraldic animals and birds came into use during the Middle Ages; the eighteenth and nineteenth centuries produced embroideries that reflected the everyday life of the people. Ancient images became magical and mythical symbols which, in turn, came to be used as decorative ornamentation.

The Slavic use of color is unique. While bright colors predominate, there are many examples of embroidery with extremely subtle pastel and delicate shades. The Slavs did not follow the color-wheel concept of color use as was done in the West. The one color used above all in Slavonic design is red. The Russian word *krasny* means red, but it also means beautiful. The origins of the Russian association of red with beautiful are lost in antiquity and have nothing to do with the present regime. In Old Russia it was not unusual to refer to a pretty girl as a "red" girl, regardless of her skin or hair color. After red, the most-often-used colors are bright blue, yellow, and green. In addition to all shadings of these four colors, all the other colors of the rainbow were used, sometimes in combinations that would not immediately occur to those used to the needlework of Western Europe.

Having grown up with a Russian mother and grandmother, and having spent my life surrounded by the paintings of my artist grandfather, I have always been in love with Slavic art. It wasn't until I discovered the joy of various kinds of needlework and embroidery that I found a practical application of this marvelous heritage.

The large amount of land inhabited by the peoples of the Slavic countries (Russia, Poland, Czechoslovakia, Yugoslavia, Bulgaria, and for our purposes, Hungary and Roumania) gave them access to many different influences that can be seen in their art. The needlework of these countries developed without the workers' knowledge of the more familiar Western forms of stitchery. The Slavonic woman looking for designs to be used in her embroidery was influenced by the factors already mentioned and by Byzantium and the Far East centuries before these styles were brought to Western Europe by the Crusaders.

The designs in this book are drawn from sources to be found in museums and from those that have become part of the traditional folk costumes of the various regions. Because they developed without contact with the elaborate embroideries of France, Italy, and other Western countries, they retain a simplicity and clarity of design that are not only refreshing and colorful, but that fit into our modern interiors and look new and original when used to decorate simple clothing styles.

Each of the designs in this book is presented with the specific project for which it was created, but they should fire your imagination in many ways to go on and use them for projects of your own. The embroidery designs given for use on linens can be applied to clothing and vice versa. Color combinations are included with each project, but these can also be switched around and used wherever wanted.

I hope that this book will introduce you to a whole world of design that has been explored very little in the West and is far too beautiful to be ignored any longer.

Before You Start

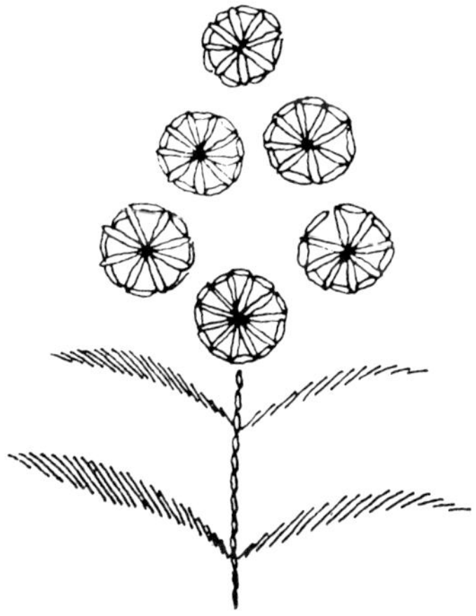

There are two basic forms of embroidery in this book. The first is free-form embroidery. Nowadays this is often referred to as crewel embroidery, but the term *crewel* actually applies to the wool. Several of these projects have been done with wool, but many of them have been done with cotton threads; therefore I will refer to this kind of stitchery as free-form embroidery. In this form the design of the embroidery is drawn directly on the fabric.

The second form of embroidery is cross stitch, which follows the threads of the background fabric, and the designs thus make geometric shapes. Cross stitch can be worked in woolen or cotton threads. To make cross-stitch embroidery authentic it should be worked on a fabric with the weft and warp threads the same size and woven evenly. It can also be done on other kinds of woven fabric with the use of needlepoint penelope (double-mesh) canvas. This will be described in the following pages.

FABRICS

For the free-form embroidery projects almost any kind of woven fabric can be used as long as it is sturdy enough to support extensive embroidery. You will, of course, have to keep in mind the nature of the object being made. A wall hanging does not have to be washable, but place mats and tablecloths do. Very sheer fabrics will not be any good, as threads carried on the back of the work will show from the front. Most of the fabrics used in the projects are white, off-white, or ecru, as these were the colors of the fabrics most often used in the Slavic countries. But there is no reason not to use bright or dark colors that contrast well with the colors of the threads used for the embroidery.

For cross-stitch embroidery the two even-weave fabrics I recommend are Aida cloth, which comes in different size weaves, and Hardanger cloth. Both of these fabrics come in white and beige. If you have any difficulties obtaining either of these fabrics (which you may, as they have not been very popular until lately), see the list of suppliers in the back of the book for the address of the company that is distributing these fabrics in North America. I have also listed some of the stores in Great Britain that carry these fabrics. There are other even-weave fabrics, such as monk's cloth, which would serve for cross-stitch embroidery, but almost all of them are manufactured in Europe and are nearly impossible to find in North America. If you do find them, either in America or in Europe, by all means use them. Remember, when looking for fabric for cross-stitch embroidery the key words are "even weave."

Cross-stitch embroidery can also be done on any woven fabric with the use of a piece of penelope or double-mesh needlepoint canvas. Center the canvas over the area to be embroidered and baste it diagonally to the background fabric. Do the embroidery making the crosses with each stitch diagonally over the double mesh of the canvas and through the fabric. Be careful not to catch the canvas in the stitches. When you have completed the design remove the basting holding the canvas and pull out the horizontal threads of the canvas. Then pull out the vertical threads, using tweezers to pull the individual threads if necessary. The size of the mesh of the canvas will determine the size of the finished cross stitch.

THREADS AND YARNS

These designs can be worked in either cotton embroidery thread or wool yarn. There are three kinds of cotton thread that can be used: six-strand embroidery floss; matte cotton thread (called *retours à broder*); and cotton perlé, which is available in three thicknesses.

The woolen yarns are Persian yarn separated into one strand or special yarn meant for crewel embroidery. Smooth needlepoint yarn cannot be used.

One word of caution about woolen yarns: If you use a brand other than that recommended with these projects you must test it first to be sure the color doesn't run. This particularly applies to bright colors such as red. In order to test it take a four-inch square of white or off-white linen and sew a strand of the red yarn doubled over in a row of back stitches. Soak the piece of linen in cold water until it is thoroughly wet. Remove it and let it dry flat, away from the sun or direct heat. After the sample is completely dry carefully cut out the row of stitching and remove all of the cut thread. Brush any stray fibers off the fabric. If you are left with a line of pinkish color on the fabric, don't use the yarn. It will run and make it impossible to clean or block the finished embroidery properly.

NEEDLES

For free-form embroidery use crewel or chenille needles. They are most often available in sizes 18, 20, and 22 with the larger number being the smaller and finer needle. I prefer chenille needles, as they have longer eyes and are shorter and therefore easier to control.

For cross-stitch embroidery on a finely woven fabric such as Hardanger cloth, crewel or chenille needles in a small size are fine. For use on Aida cloth tapestry needles, which come in the same sizes as the crewel and chenille needles but have blunt points, are perfect, as the needle passes between the fibers of fabric in the holes naturally formed at the right angles of the fibers.

EMBROIDERY HOOPS

Most of the projects in this book must be worked with an embroidery hoop. These hoops are available in all sizes from hand-held hoops 4″ in diameter to large hoops with a 10″ or 12″ diameter, which come with their own stands. These can stand on a table or the floor, depending on the height of the stand. There is another kind of hoop which fastens on the side of a table. All the hoops made on stands are made of highly varnished wood.

Hand-held hoops are made of wood, plastic, or metal. Do not use the metal ones, as they can damage and/or discolor the fabric. The different size hoops serve different purposes. The size of the hoop needed is determined by the size of the fabric being used. For small pieces, such as the sections of a garment that are embroidered before the garment is sewn together, you will need the small hand-held hoops. For larger pieces the 10″ or 12″ hoops with stands are ideal, as they allow you to use both hands for the stitching.

Square frames and artists' stretchers can be used for embroidery, but they must be the same size as the piece of embroidery. They are difficult to handle and I find the time needed in sewing the piece of embroidery to the frame unnecessary for the kind of work shown in this book.

To use a hoop, start by adjusting the screw so that the inner hoop fits snugly into the outer hoop. You cannot alter the adjustment after the fabric is in the hoop.

Place the fabric over the inner hoop, centering the design to be embroidered, and place the outer hoop gently down around all the edges. Be sure that the fabric is tightly stretched when the outer hoop is in place. If the fabric is not as tight as a drum, or if it loosens while you are working on it, remove the outer ring, tighten the adjustment screw, and replace it.

Even with hand-held hoops always stab the needle in and out of the fabric and never try to take more than one stitch at a time. You are not sewing, you are *embroidering*, and this difference in working will show on the finished piece.

Always use hoops when doing free-form embroidery. They are not necessary with most of the cross-stitch embroidery as long as you are careful not to pull the thread too tight or to leave it so loose that it forms loops or doesn't lie flat.

Plate 1 Child's dress with Yugoslavian embroidery. Pages 30–33.

Plate 2 Long apron with Czechoslovakian embroidery. Pages 34–37.

Plate 3 Front of vest with Roumanian-inspired embroidery. Pages 50–55.

Plate 4 Back view of the vest.

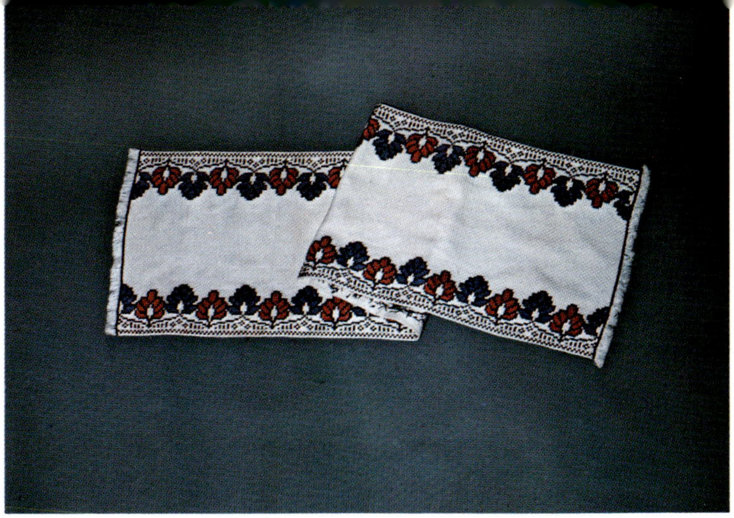

Plate 5 Table runner with Russian cross-stitch design. Pages 60–63.

Plate 6 Coaster mats with Russian cross-stitch design. Pages 64–65.

Plate 7 Place mat with cross-stitched Yugoslavian design. Pages 70–73.

Plate 8 Place mat with counted-stitch Yugoslavian design. Pages 74–75.

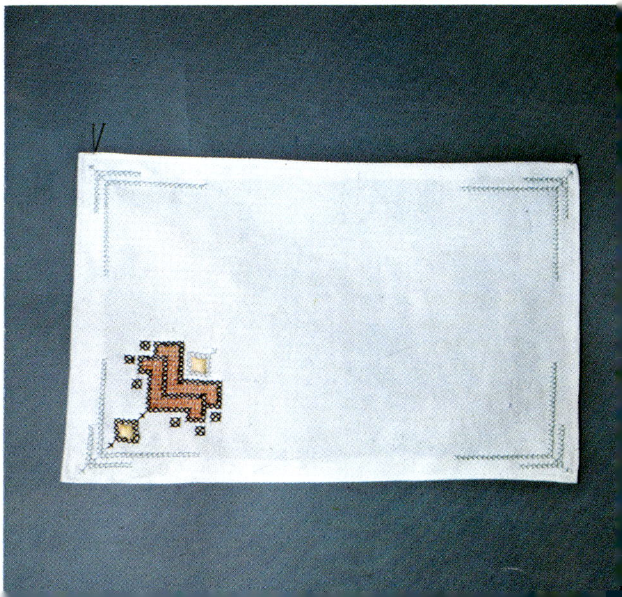

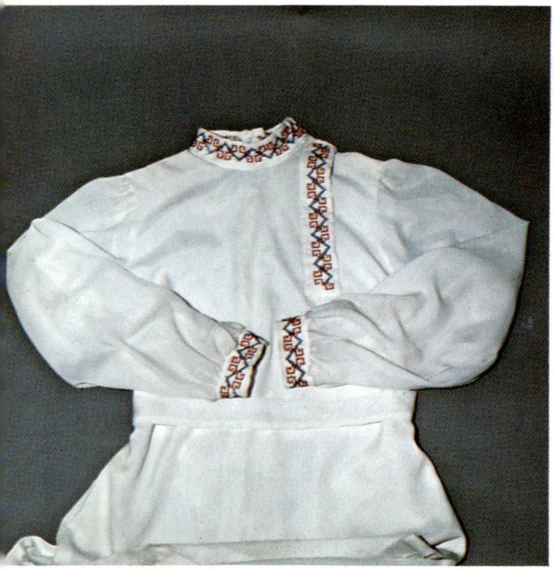

Plate 9 Russian cross-stitch design on a ready-made blouse. Pages 77–79.

Plate 10 Russian tablecloth and napkin. Courtesy Lucy Kortchmar. Pages 80–85.

Plate 11 Russian peasant apron with counted-stitch embroidery in shades of blue and white, with crocheted hem; nineteenth century. Courtesy Lucy Kortchmar. Page 90.

The instructions for each project will tell where a hoop is needed, and what size hoop to use.

HOW TO TRANSFER THE DESIGN TO THE FABRIC

Cross-stitch designs do not have to be marked on the fabric. The size of the individual stitch, and therefore the overall design, depends on the size of the mesh of the even-weave fabric. The cross stitch can cover one thread of the fabric or multiples of two; that is, a stitch can cover two threads both vertically and horizontally, or four, or six, and so on. Just be sure that the completed cross stitch forms a square. Follow the chart given with the project for the placement of the stitches. The mark in each square on the graph stands for one stitch. The marks may differ to indicate different colors; these are shown in the key given with the chart. Start the design at one corner and continue with the pattern of the stitches, changing the color of the thread where needed. For those of you who like needlepoint, the charts given for the cross-stitch designs can be followed on needlepoint canvas, filling in the background with white or ecru yarn.

TRACING THE DESIGN

There are several ways of tracing the design of a free-form embroidery onto the fabric.

First you will have to enlarge the design by the use of squares given behind the design on a piece of tracing paper, making the squares as large as necessary. For example, if the design is to be four times larger than given, make each square four times as large as those in the book. Copy the design from the book onto the tracing paper, square by square.

METHODS USED TO TRACE THE DESIGN

1. *Dressmaker's Carbon Paper*

Buy a package of dressmaker's carbon paper with different colors of paper. *Do not* try to use ordinary carbon paper.

Divide the fabric into four sections (in half and in half again) for square pieces, or determine the center of the fabric where the design will go and fold it there. Spread the fabric out smoothly with the right side facing you on a flat surface. Tape the edges down with masking tape. Note: Be sure not to use the top of a good table or other furniture, as the tracing wheel will leave permanent marks.

Use white or yellow carbon paper for dark-colored fabrics or blue, green, or any other color for white or beige fabrics. Place the carbon paper on the fabric with the shiny side down. Fold the traced design in half and in half again to determine the center. Place the tracing paper on top of the carbon, lining up the center of the design with the fold marks. Hold the tracing paper in place with weights. Use the tracing wheel and trace the design through the carbon paper onto the fabric. Bear down very hard on the tracing wheel and lift the edge of the carbon periodically to make sure that you are transferring the design.

2. *Transfer Pencils*

Pink transfer pencils enable you to make your own iron-on transfers. These pencils are sold by mail-order needle-craft supply stores and in some needle-craft stores and departments.

After you have made a drawing of the design on tracing paper, turn it over and go over the original pencil lines with the transfer pencil. The design is drawn on the *back* because it will reverse itself when you iron it onto the fabric. Before you iron the design onto the fabric, make a test line or two on a separate piece of tracing paper and iron it onto a scrap of the fabric with the iron set for wool heat and with no water in it so that there will be no steam or accidental dripping.

Lift the iron and press down on the paper; do not slide the iron along the fabric.

The transfer pencils work very well on natural fiber fabrics (cotton and linen). They are not advisable for use on synthetics, as the amount of heat required to transfer the pencil line to a synthetic is too hot for the fabric itself.

One word of caution: Sharpen the pencil well away from any fabric (including the clothes you are wearing), as the pencil sharpenings can cover everything with a dusting of bright pink.

3. Net

If you plan to use a fabric with a nubbly surface for your embroidery use a piece of net and a waterproof marking pen to transfer the design. Be sure before you start that the marking pen is really waterproof. Test it by making a line or two on a scrap of the fabric, let the ink dry, and then soak the marked fabric in cold water for ten or fifteen minutes. If the ink does not run or wash off you know that it is completely waterproof.

Trace the design on the net with the marking pen. Pin the net to the fabric, centering the design, and trace the design over the net and the fabric. The ink will pass through the holes of the net directly onto the fabric.

Color

When it comes to choosing color schemes for these designs forget anything you have learned about color wheels, complementary colors, and so on. The people who have created Slavic folk art never took an art course in their lives and the Western use of color is unknown to them.

The strongest outside influence on Slavic embroidery came from the East, with different areas of the Orient affecting those parts of Russia and the other Eastern European countries closest to them geographically. Some Chinese influence can be seen in those areas invaded by the Mongols under Genghis Khan. A far greater influence came from Byzantium, from which the Russian form of Christianity was taken, and from the Moslem countries of the Middle East. For example, the embroidery of the Caucasian peoples shows the influence of the needlework of bordering Turkey and Persia. In many cases the difference between the needlework of some

Slavic countries and that of certain sections of the Middle East can be seen only by experts.

Despite the forces of foreign influence on some examples of Slavic embroidery, the long isolation of these people and their inability to travel (for economic or political reasons) gave rise to a unique form of needlework that is found only in this part of the world.

There are some colors that show up again and again in all the work of the various Slavic countries, but every time there seems to be a rule of color selection, one finds examples of work that break the rule. As mentioned, the most-often-used color is red—not only a clear, bright red, but various shades from dark brown-red to a blue-red that comes close to being a shade of magenta. The other most-used colors are blue (and various shades of blue), green, yellow, orange, purple, and black. As you can see from a glimpse at the photographs of the projects, these colors are often used in combinations, but many of the most superb examples of needlework are monochromatic (several shades of the same color) or worked completely in one color.

As a contrast to the bright colors mentioned, the same colors in pastel shades can be combined and substituted for any of the projects. The pastel colors will give a different look to the work and still be authentic.

Before deciding on the colors of the threads for a particular project, first choose the background fabric. The color of the background will influence your choice of colors for the threads. Almost all the examples of Slavic embroidery that can be found in museums (and those being made today) are worked on a white or off-white fabric. There are some exceptions, with bright red or blue used as a background. For these projects I have mainly used off-white fabrics, but this is not a strict rule, as can be seen in the child's dress and the long skirt.

If you don't want to stick to the colors used in a particular project, take your background fabric and lay a few skeins of different-colored thread on it and decide whether you like the effect of the colors, not only with each other but also against the color of the fabric. For the linens and decorative pillows, take into consideration the colors of the room in which they will be used.

For clothing, one of the most effective uses of color to be seen in Slavic embroidery is that of no color at all. I am referring to blouses made of white fabric and embroidered in elaborate patterns with white thread.

Stitches

The stitches marked with an asterisk (*) in this list should be done with the fabric held in an embroidery hoop. They should not be *sewn* in; rather, they should be *stabbed* in and out of the fabric, using a separate movement on the top and underside of the fabric. The drawings show the stitches being sewn, but this is only to simplify the instructions.

Start with a piece of thread no longer than 18″ Thread the needle and tie a small knot in one end of the thread. Never tie both ends of the thread together. If you want to use more than one strand of the thread pass both ends of the thread through the needle and tie the ends of the strands together as shown. When the thread you are working with is about 5″ long, end off the thread by taking it to the wrong side of the fabric, pass the needle under a few threads of the previously made stitches, and make a small knot. Cut off the thread close to the knot.

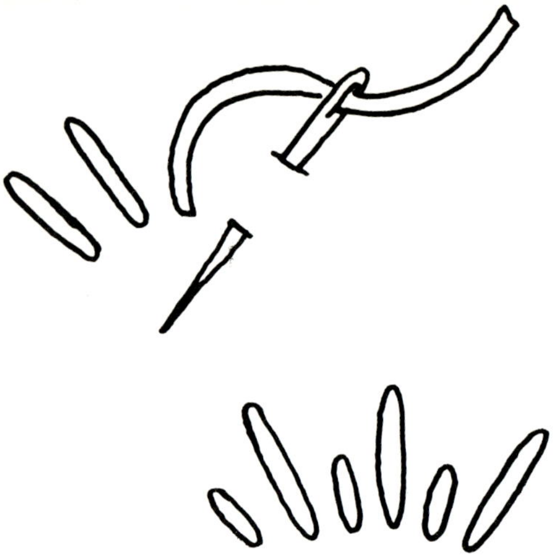

Straight stitch

*1. *Straight Stitch*

Bring the needle up from the wrong side of the fabric, bring it down, forming a stitch of the desired length, and bring the needle up at the beginning of the next stitch. Don't pull the thread too tight or it will pucker the fabric, but don't leave it too loose or it will catch on things. These stitches are often made in different lengths.

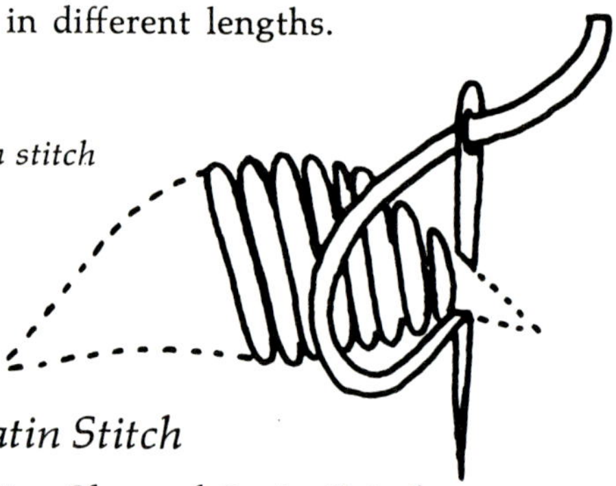

Satin stitch

2. *Satin Stitch*

**a. Slanted Satin Stitch*

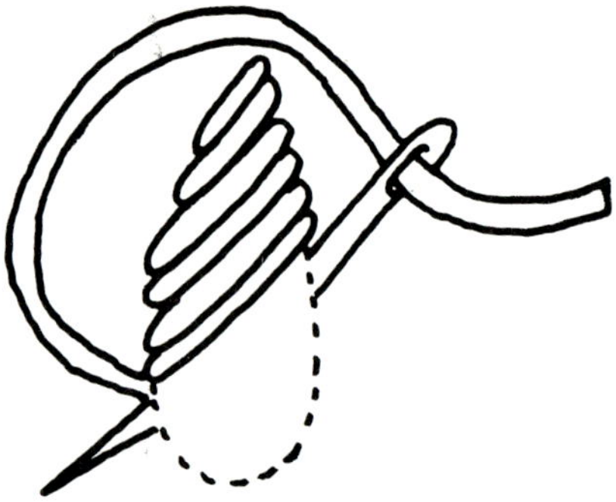

Slanted satin stitch

Start in the center of the shape and bring the needle up from the wrong side of the fabric. Make a row of straight stitches next to each other, keeping the stitches slanting in the same direction. Be sure to follow the outline of the shape exactly. Do not make the stitches too long or they will be pulled out of shape.

b. Counted Satin Stitch

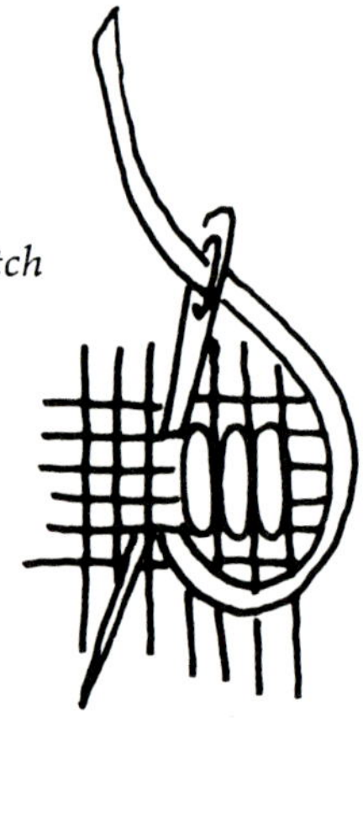

Counted satin stitch

Start the stitch from right to left or left to right and pass the stitch over the number of threads called for. These stitches can be worked horizontally or diagonally as well as vertically.

*3. *Stem Stitch*

Bring the needle up at the start of the stem, down, and then back up halfway between the start and finish of the first stitch, holding the thread to the left of the needle. Start the next stitch away from the first stitch along the line and bring the needle down. Bring the needle up at the end of the previous stitch. Repeat, keeping the thread to the left of the needle.

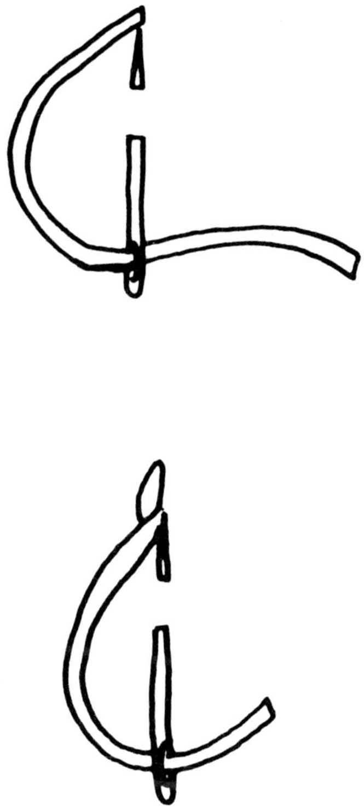

Stem stitch

*4. *Back Stitch*

Bring the needle up one stitch length along the line and bring the needle back to the beginning of the line; pull the needle to the wrong side of the fabric. Start the next stitch one stitch length ahead of the previous stitch and repeat. Make all the stitches the same length. The next two stitches are counted and are to be done on evenweave fabric. They can be done without an embroidery hoop as long as you keep the tension of the stitches even, not pulling them too tight or leaving them so loose that they don't lie neatly on the fabric.

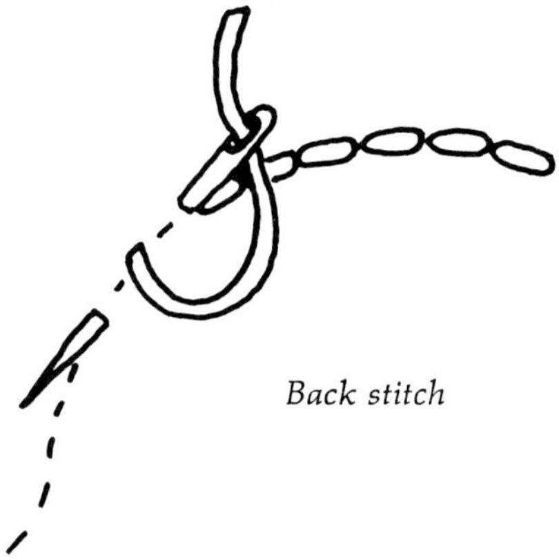

Back stitch

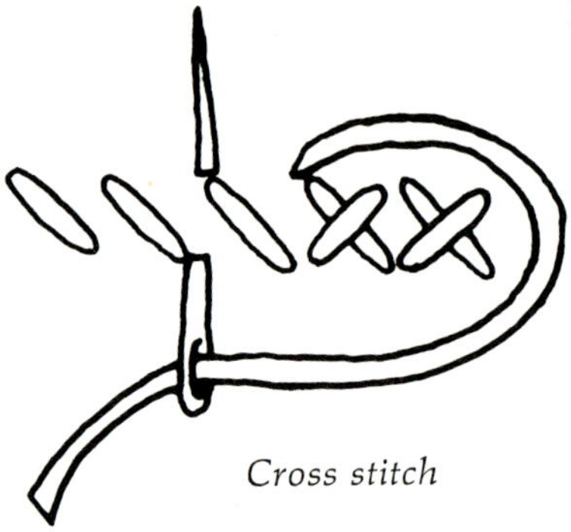

Cross stitch

5. *Cross Stitch*

This stitch is made in two journeys. Bring the needle up at the lower right-hand side and cross over the required number of the threads to the left; bring the needle down and up again the required number of threads below the first stitch and repeat for the length of the row. For the return journey repeat the first row by forming the top stitch from left to right as shown. Be sure that all the top stitches lie in the same direction.

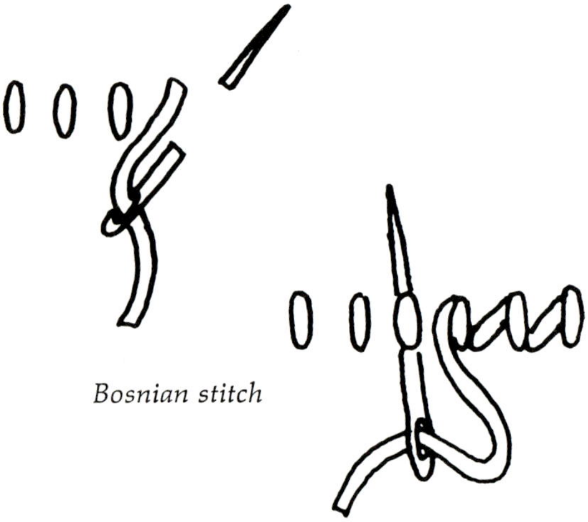

Bosnian stitch

6. *Bosnian Stitch*

This stitch is also made in two journeys. Working from left to right make a row of vertical stitches covering two threads and two threads apart. For the return journey pass the needle under the first right-hand stitch and diagonally across to the next stitch, passing the needle under the stitch as shown.

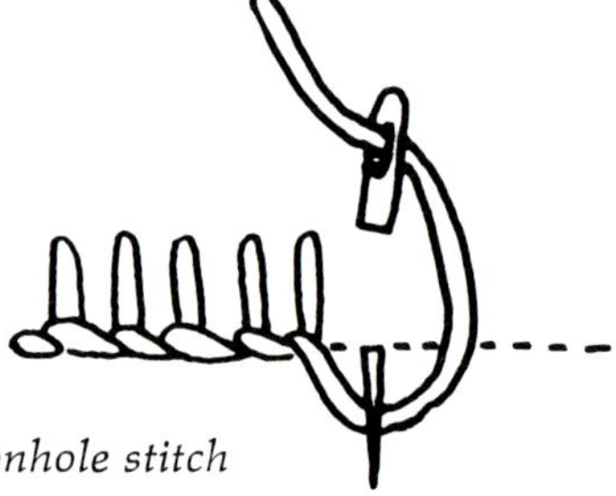

Buttonhole stitch

7. *Buttonhole Stitch*

Bring the thread up at the lower line, insert the needle at the upper line, and make a straight downward stitch with the thread under the needle. Pull the needle and form a loop. Be careful not to pull too tightly.

*8. *Chain Stitch*

Bring the needle up at the start of the line. Bring the thread to the left and hold it with your finger, forming a loop. Insert the needle back where it came up, bring the needle up a short distance with the thread under the needle, and draw the thread gently, forming the first chain stitch. Make the rest of the stitches the same way, always inserting the needle exactly where it came up. Make all the stitches the same size.

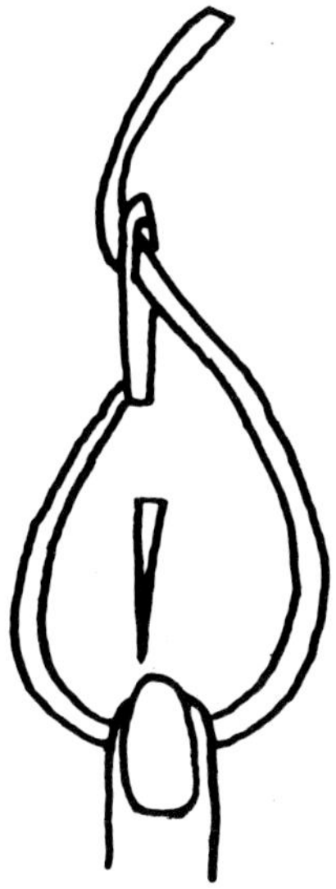

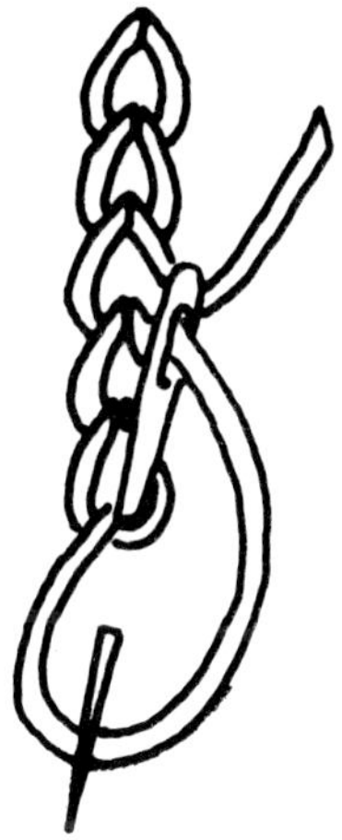

Chain stitch

*9. *Detached Chain Stitch*

Make a single chain stitch and fasten the loop with a small stitch. The length of the stitch taken will determine the shape of the final stitch. A small stitch will make a rounded shape, a longer stitch will form an oval.

Detached chain stitch

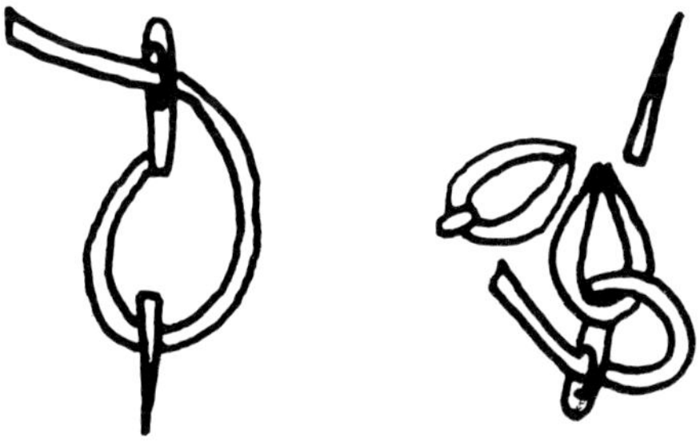

*10. *Long and Short Stitch*

Make a row of long and short satin stitches side by side. The shorter stitch should be three-quarters of the length of the longer one. Make another row of long and short satin stitches so that the second row meshes with the stitches in the first row.

Long and short stitch

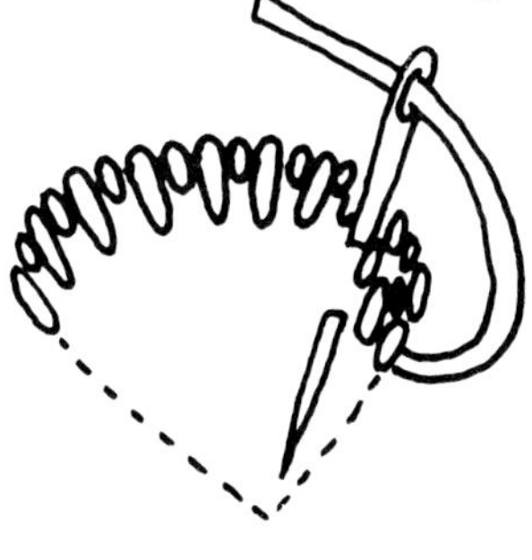

11. Herringbone Stitch

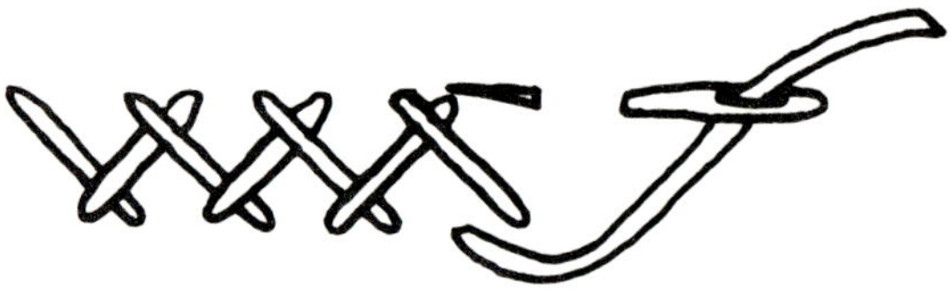

Herringbone stitch

Starting on the left side, bring the needle up on the lower line, insert it in the upper line a little to the right, and take a small stitch to the left with the thread below the needle. Insert the needle on the lower line a little to the right and make a small stitch to the left with the thread above the needle. Repeat, keeping the stitches the same length and the spaces between them even.

12. *Laidwork Tied with Crossbars

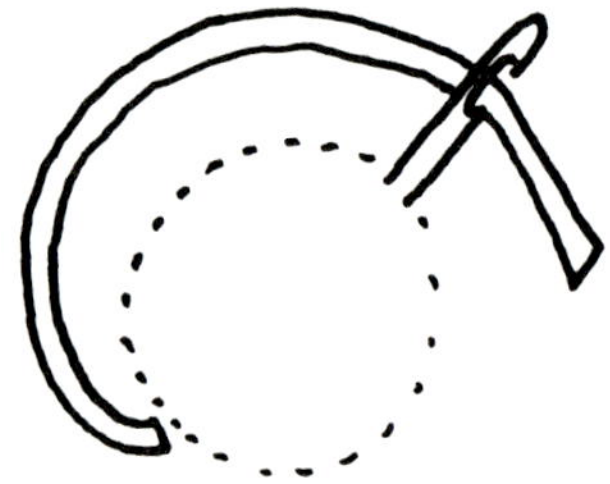

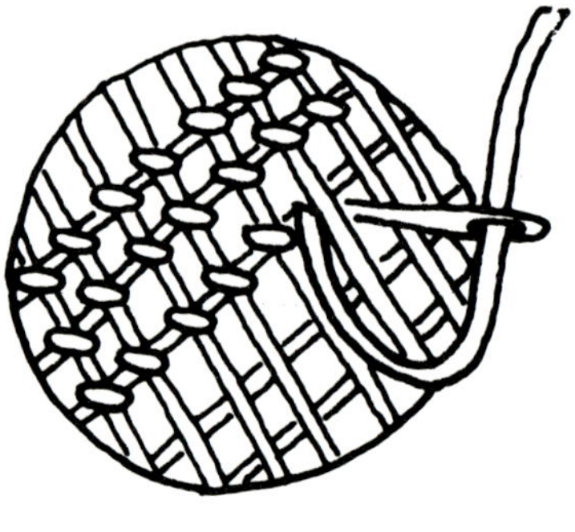

Laidwork tied with crossbars

Bring the needle up at the lower left and make a long diagonal stitch. Bring the needle up a short distance away from the first stitch on the upper right side and make a parallel stitch. Repeat until the space is filled. Repeat with the second row of stitches crossing over the first until the space is filled. With another color thread make small horizontal stitches over the diagonal stitches where they intersect.

13. *Weaving Stitch

Make a row of long stitches the same length, a small distance away from each other. With another color thread and a tapestry needle bring the needle up at the side of the previous stitches. Weave under and over the stitches and bring the needle down at the other side. Come up a short distance below the stitch just made and weave it in the other direction. Repeat until the motif is finished.

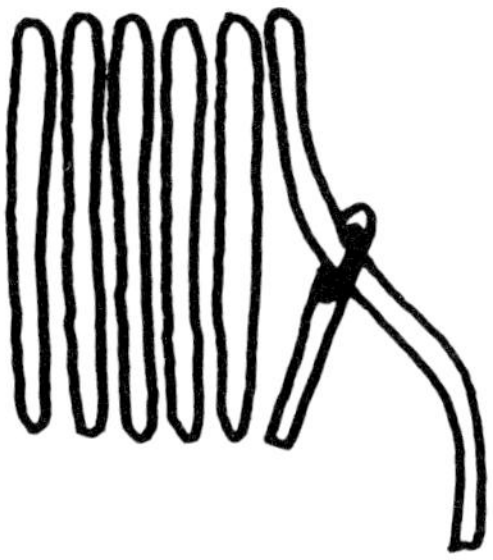

Weaving stitch

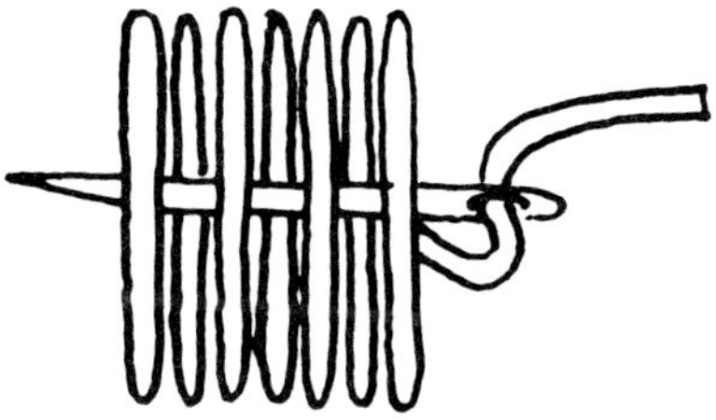

14. *Fly Stitch

Bring the needle up at the left and down to the right and above the place where you came up. Bring the needle up below the place where the needle has been inserted with the thread under the needle. Make a small stitch over the loop.

Fly stitch

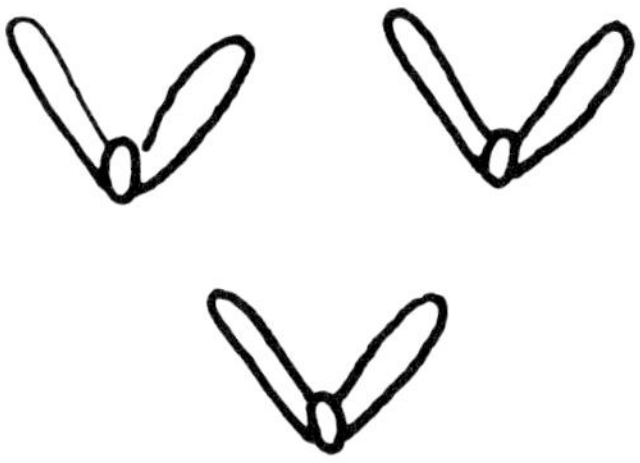

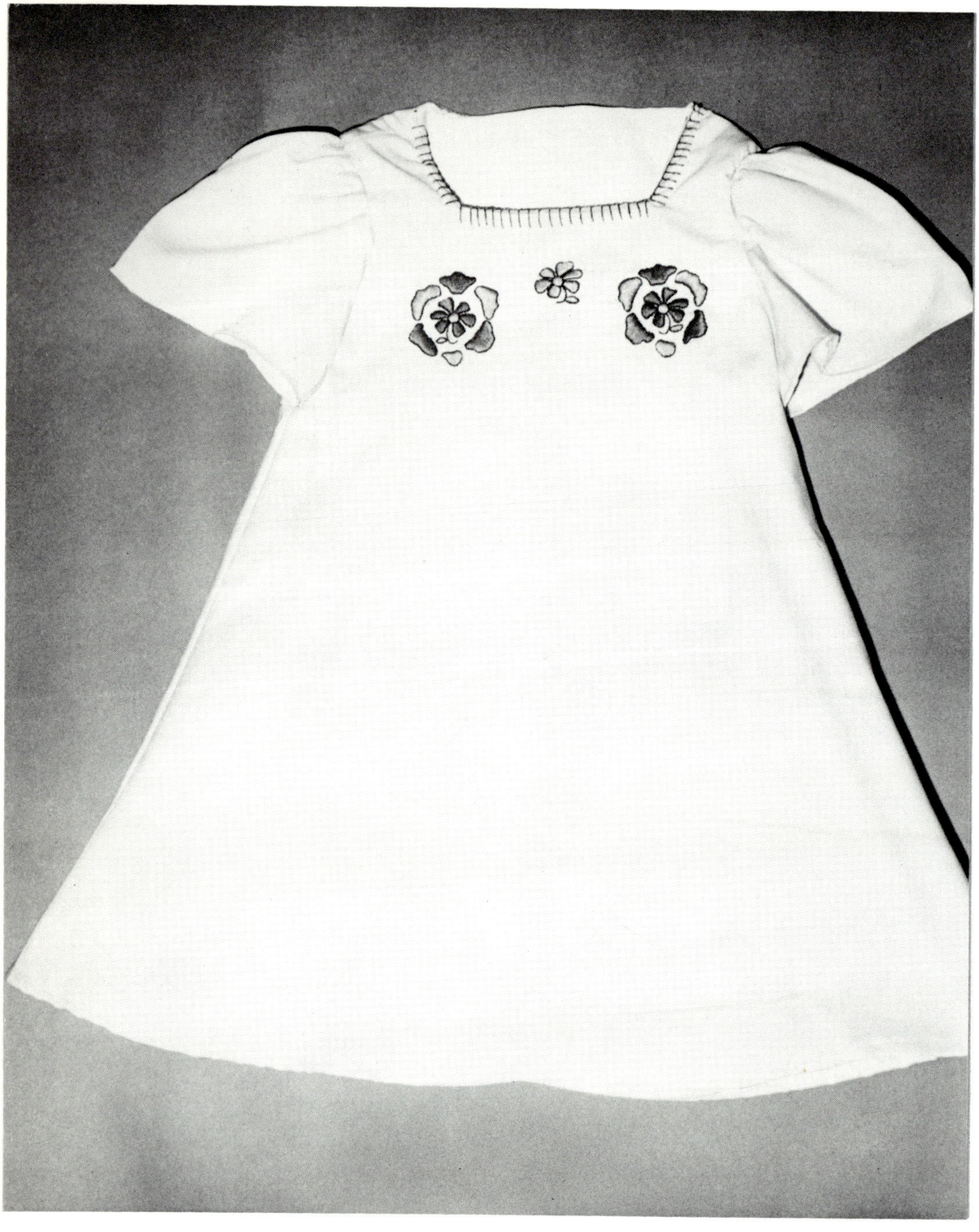

Free Form Embroidery

PROJECT I
CHILD'S DRESS

Adapted from a Yugoslavian design for the border of a shawl, these charming flowers can be used to decorate women's blouses or dresses as well as the child's dress shown here.

What you will need:

Simplicity pattern no. 6183
Lightweight cotton fabric in the length called for on the pattern envelope
Size 6 embroidery or crewel needle
Size 18 crewel needle
D.M.C. six-strand (Article 117):
334 Medium blue
470 Green
444 Yellow
309 Dark rose
Black
D.M.C. perlé size 5 (Article 116):
905 Green
4″ or 5″ embroidery hoop

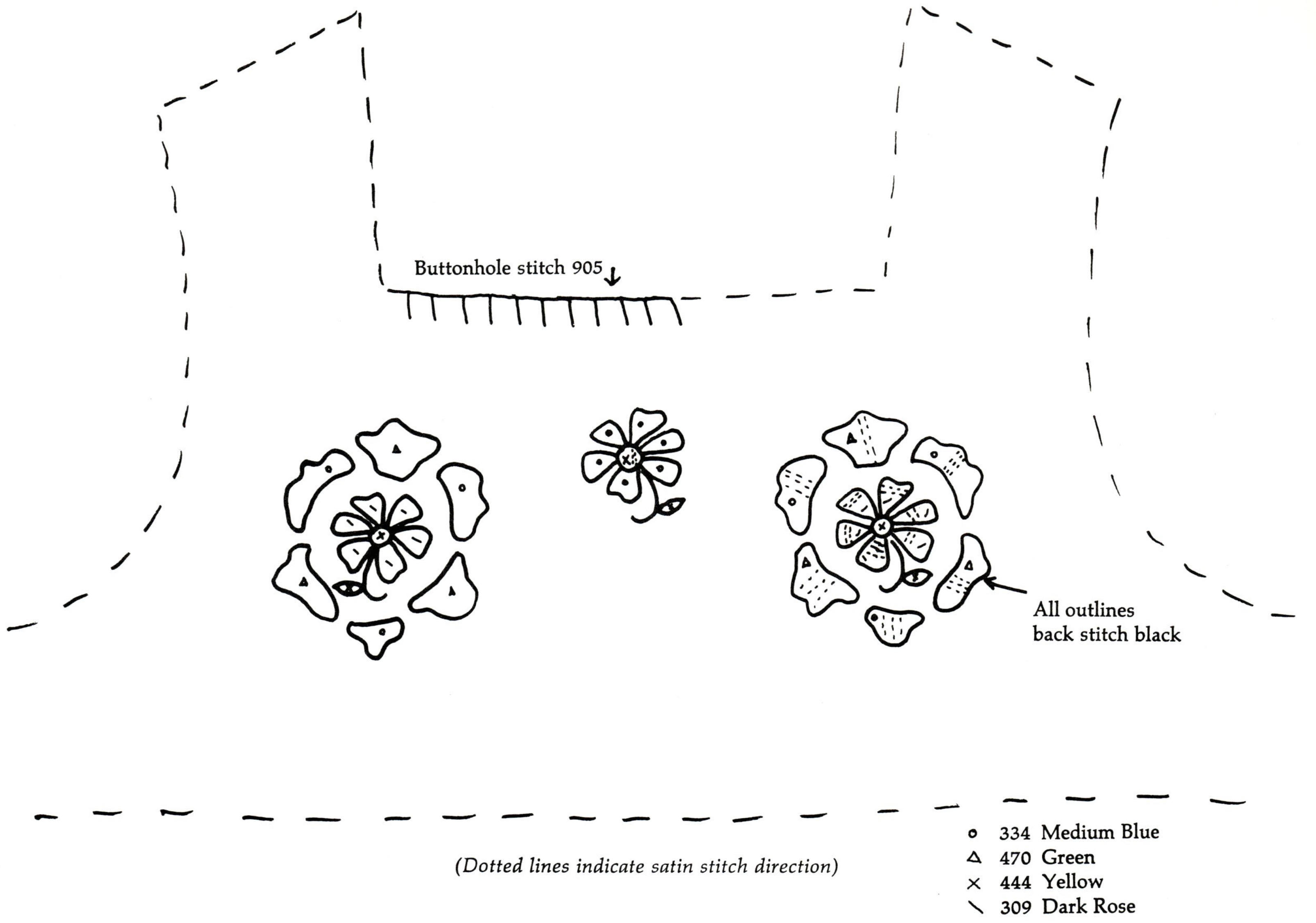
Buttonhole stitch 905
All outlines
back stitch black
(Dotted lines indicate satin stitch direction)
o 334 Medium Blue
△ 470 Green
× 444 Yellow
\ 309 Dark Rose

After cutting out the dress, transfer the design to the front bodice. Make the dress according to the pattern instructions, ignoring references to appliqué, embroidery, and trimmings.

When the dress is finished open the back zipper and center one of the flowers in the small hoop. Working with three strands of the six-strand floss and a size 6 embroidery needle, work the outlines with black thread in a back stitch. Following the diagram for color placement work the insides of the design in satin stitch using three strands of the floss throughout. When one area is finished move the hoop to the other parts of the design and finish the front embroidery as described.

With the perlé thread and size 18 crewel needle make a row of buttonhole stitches around the neckline. Do not use the hoop when making the buttonhole stitch.

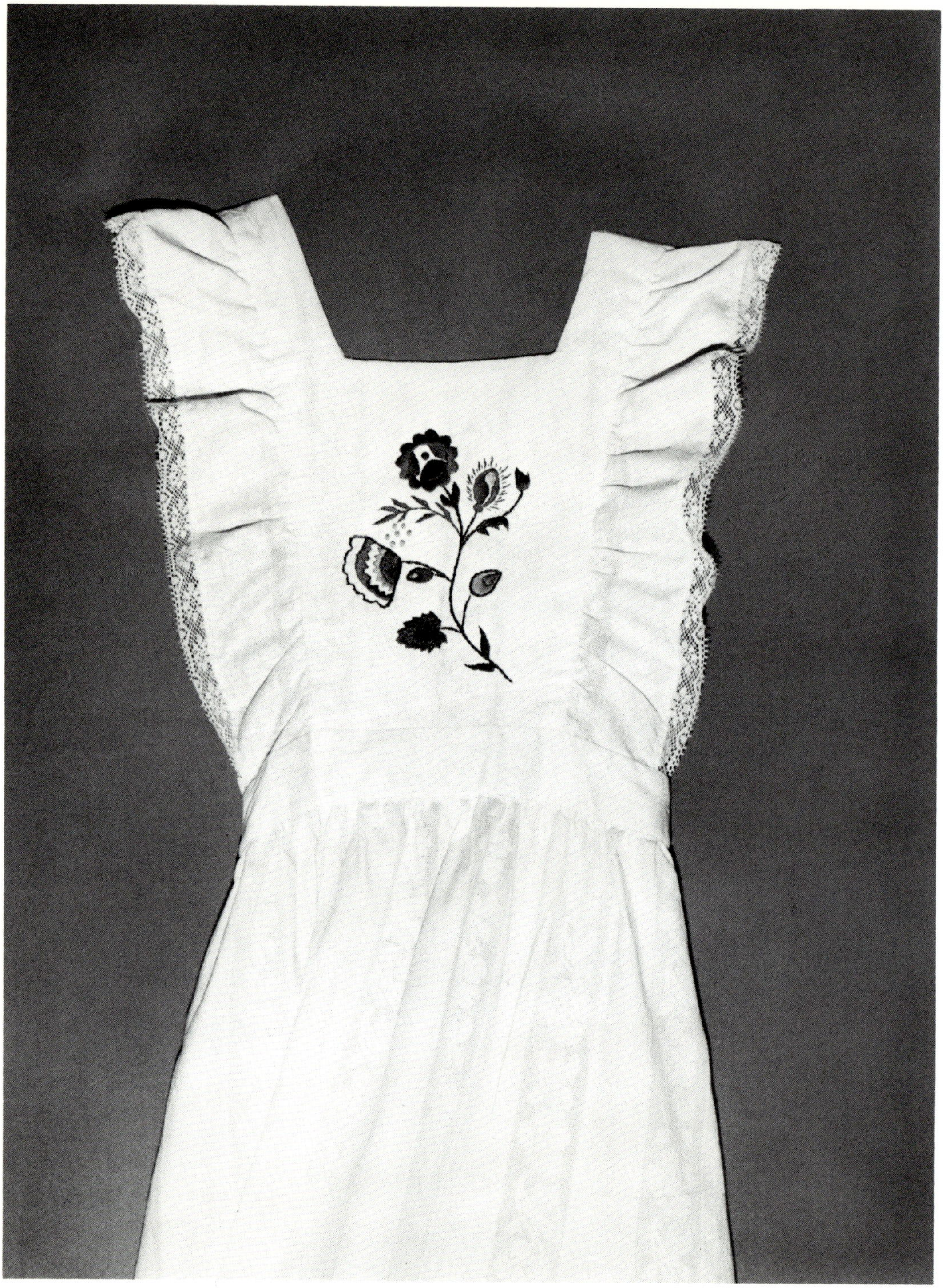

PROJECT II
LONG APRON

The delicate Czechoslovakian bouquet can be used to decorate any article of clothing.

What you will need:

Long apron, purchased ready-made or made from a pattern
10″ or 12″ embroidery hoop
Size 6 embroidery needle
Size 20 crewel or chenille needle
D.M.C. perlé size 5 (Article 116):
- 919 Rust

D.M.C. six-strand (Article 117):
- 666 Red
- 444 Yellow
- 550 Purple
- 740 Orange
- 312 Dark blue
- 905 Green
- 935 Dark green

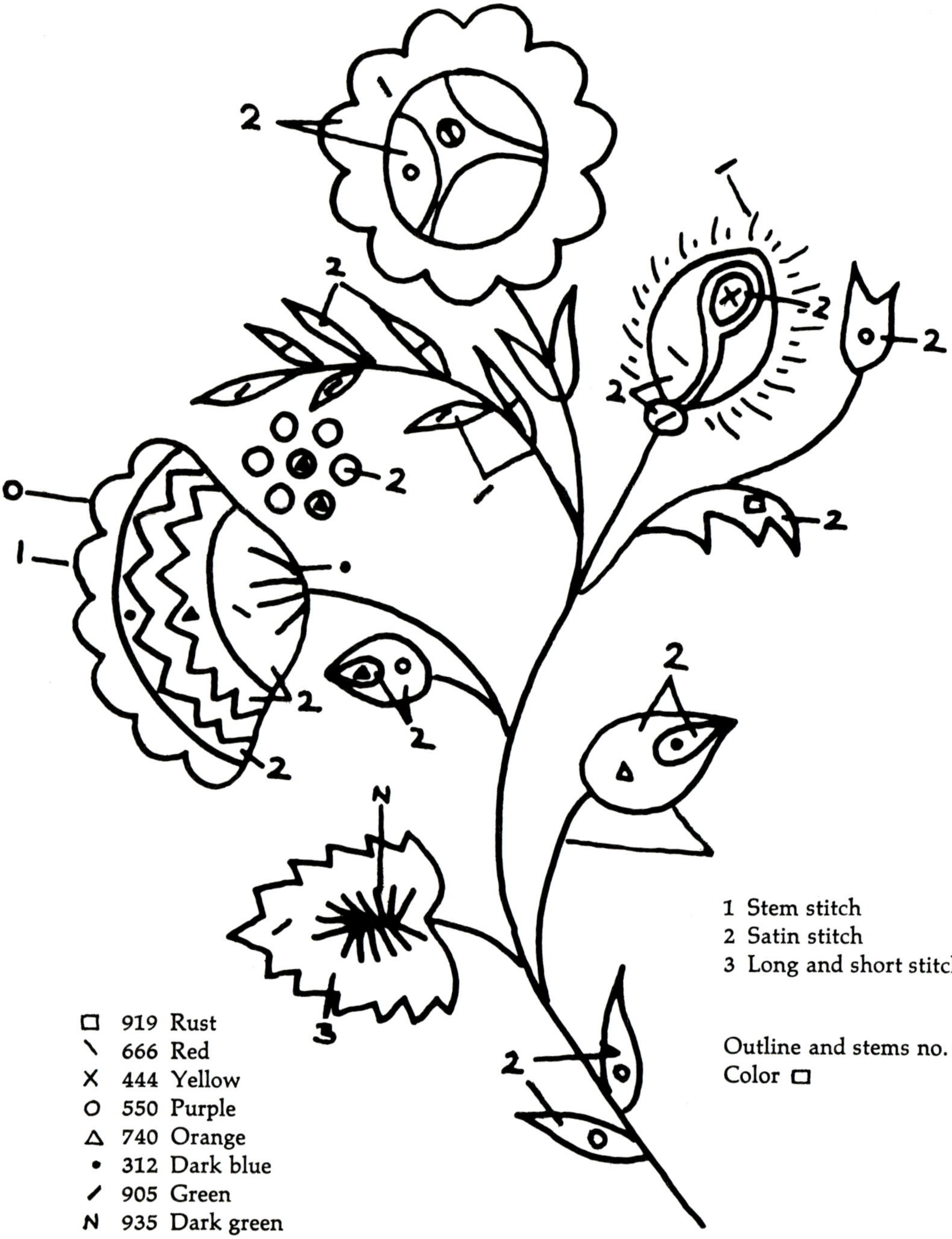

1 Stem stitch
2 Satin stitch
3 Long and short stitch

Outline and stems no. 1
Color □

□ 919 Rust
╲ 666 Red
X 444 Yellow
O 550 Purple
△ 740 Orange
• 312 Dark blue
/ 905 Green
N 935 Dark green

Transfer the design to the front of the apron. Place the fabric in the hoop, centering the design. With the pearl cotton and a size 20 crewel needle work the stems and outline of the lower right-hand bud in stem stitch. Work the rest of the design in stem stitch and satin stitch, following the diagram for stitch and color placement. Use three strands of the six-strand throughout. Work the large leaf in long and short stitch with no. 905 green, and then work the center in no. 935 dark green in satin stitch over the area already worked.

PROJECT III
HEAD SCARF

The delightful Polish flowers used to decorate this scarf can be used for all kinds of clothing and table linens, such as place mats. The herringbone stitch appears in many Polish embroideries and can almost be considered a kind of signature.

What you will need:

¾ yard of soft fabric, 36″ wide
Size 22 crewel or chenille needle
D.M.C. perlé thread (Article 116):
  Size 8—
    666 Red
    905 Green
  Size 5—
    444 Yellow
    666 Red
    797 Blue

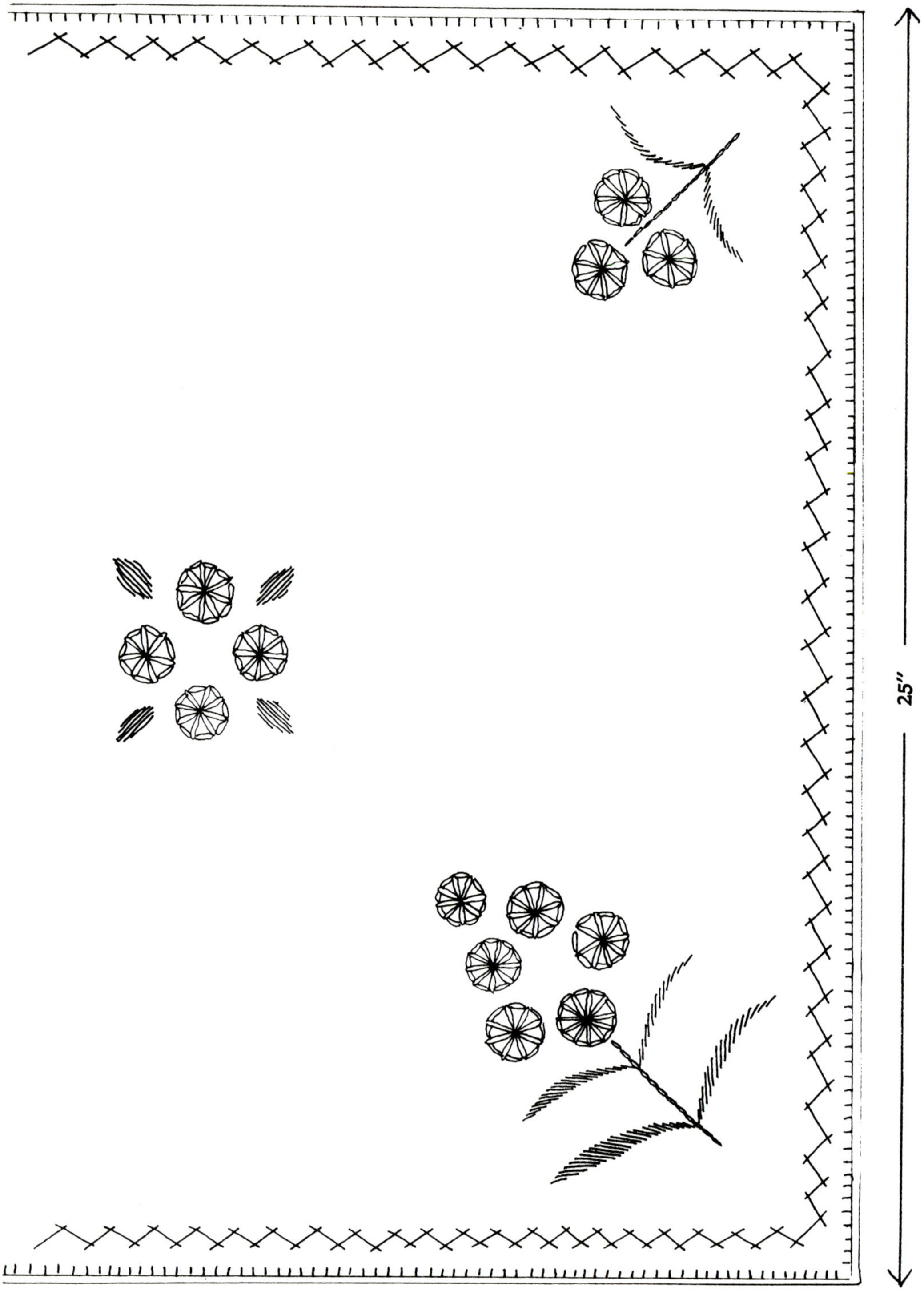
25"

Cut the fabric in a square 25½″ x 25½″. Press under ¼″ around the edges and then make another fold the same size. Stitch it down by machine or hand. Work the border stitches first, following the diagram. Fold the square in half diagonally and press lightly, then fold along the other diagonal and press. Use the creases made for the placement of the flowers and leaves, following the diagram. Mark the flowers and leaves on the fabric with tailor's chalk.

After the embroidery is finished, wash the scarf if necessary to remove the chalk marks. Press lightly on a folded terry towel with the wrong side up.

Outer border

Buttonhole stitch
D.M.C. perlé size 8
666 Red

Inner border

Herringbone stitch
D.M.C. perlé size 5
797 Blue
444 Yellow

Stems—stem stitch
Leaves—satin stitch
D.M.C. perlé size 8
905 Green

Flowers—buttonhole stitch
D.M.C. perlé size 5
666 Red
797 Blue

PROJECT IV
HUNGARIAN TABLE MAT

This mat can be used as a centerpiece on a large table or as a cover for a small circular table with the corners hanging down.

What you will need:

- Coarse linen 26″ x 26″ square
- Size 18 crewel or chenille needle
- 6″ or 10″ embroidery hoop
- Size C (2.50 European) crochet hook
- D.M.C. matte cotton (Retours à Broder, Article 89):
  - 2742 Yellow
  - 2666 Red
  - 2820 Blue
  - 2905 Green

NOTE:

Centers of all hearts 7 X tied with + crossbars

Wheels—alternate colors noted

Back stitch (9) around wheels, alternate colors noted

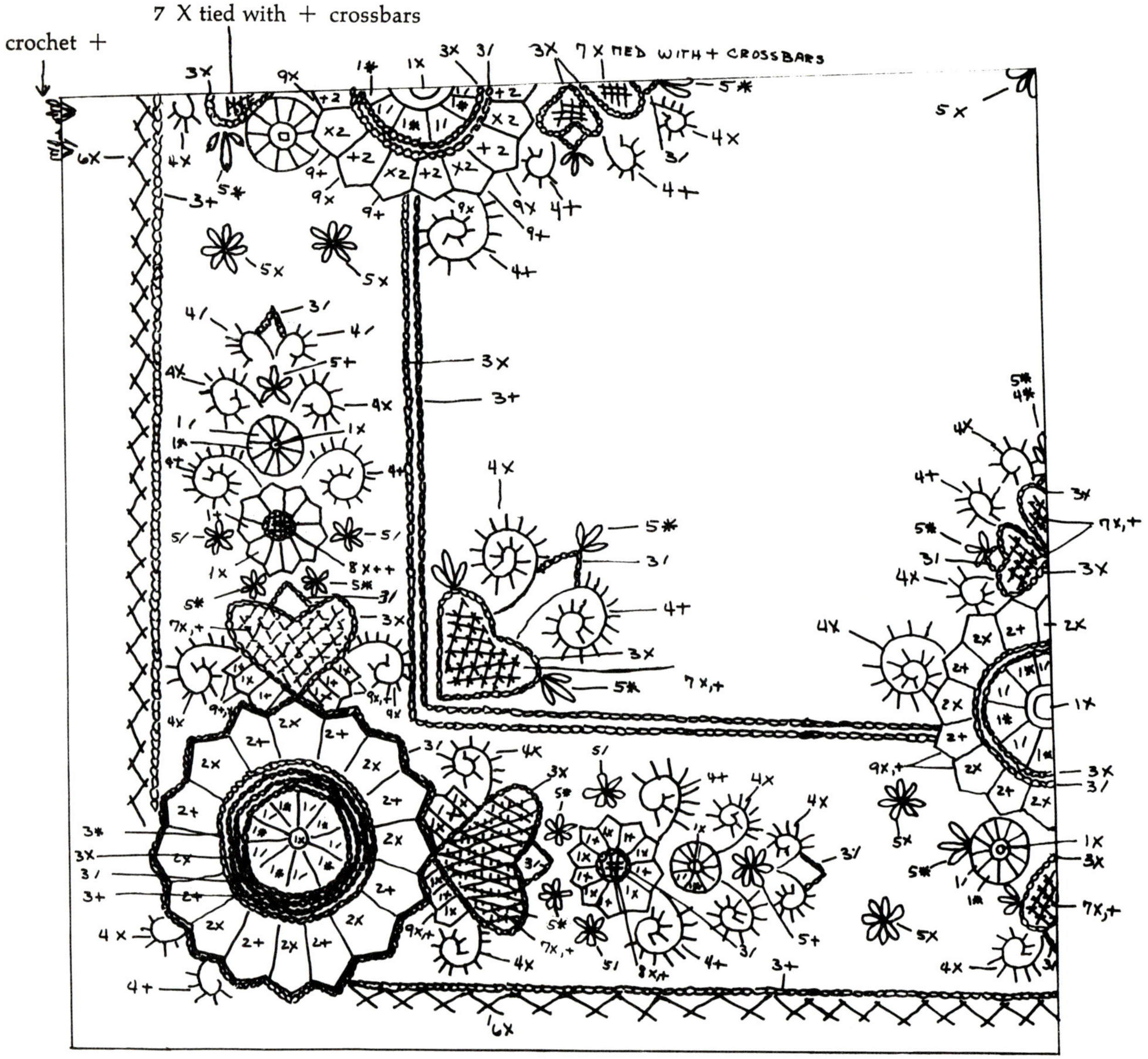

Turn under 1/4″ around all four sides and turn again. Press and sew in place on the wrong side.

Transfer the design to the fabric.

Following the diagram for color and stitch placement work the design starting in one corner. See pages 24–29 for instructions for the stitches.

When the embroidery is finished, make holes in the edge of the fabric 1/2″ apart with the size 18 crewel needle. Working in the holes with the blue thread and the crochet hook, make a row of simple crochet stitches in each one of the holes.

Make the picot stitch as follows: Make single crochet stitches until you are above one of the holes. Chain three and insert the hook into the fourth stitch from the hook, yarn over and yarn through that loop and the loop on the hook. Single crochet into the next stitch as shown.

Colors

/ Yellow
× Red
+ Blue
✱ Green

Stitches

1 Satin stitch
2 Long and short stitch
3 Chain stitch
4 Buttonhole stitch
5 Detached chain stitch
6 Herringbone stitch
7 Laidwork tied with crossbars
8 Weaving stitch
9 Back stitch

PROJECT V
LONG SKIRT

This Russian design can be used to decorate any long skirt, either ready-made or one you have made yourself.

What you will need:

Long skirt
Size 20 crewel or chenille needle
6″ or 10″ embroidery hoop
D.M.C. perlé size 5 (Article 116):
444 Yellow
666 Red
740 Orange

× 444 Yellow
\ 666 Red
Δ 740 Orange

Outline, tail feathers, feet, and crown—stem stitch

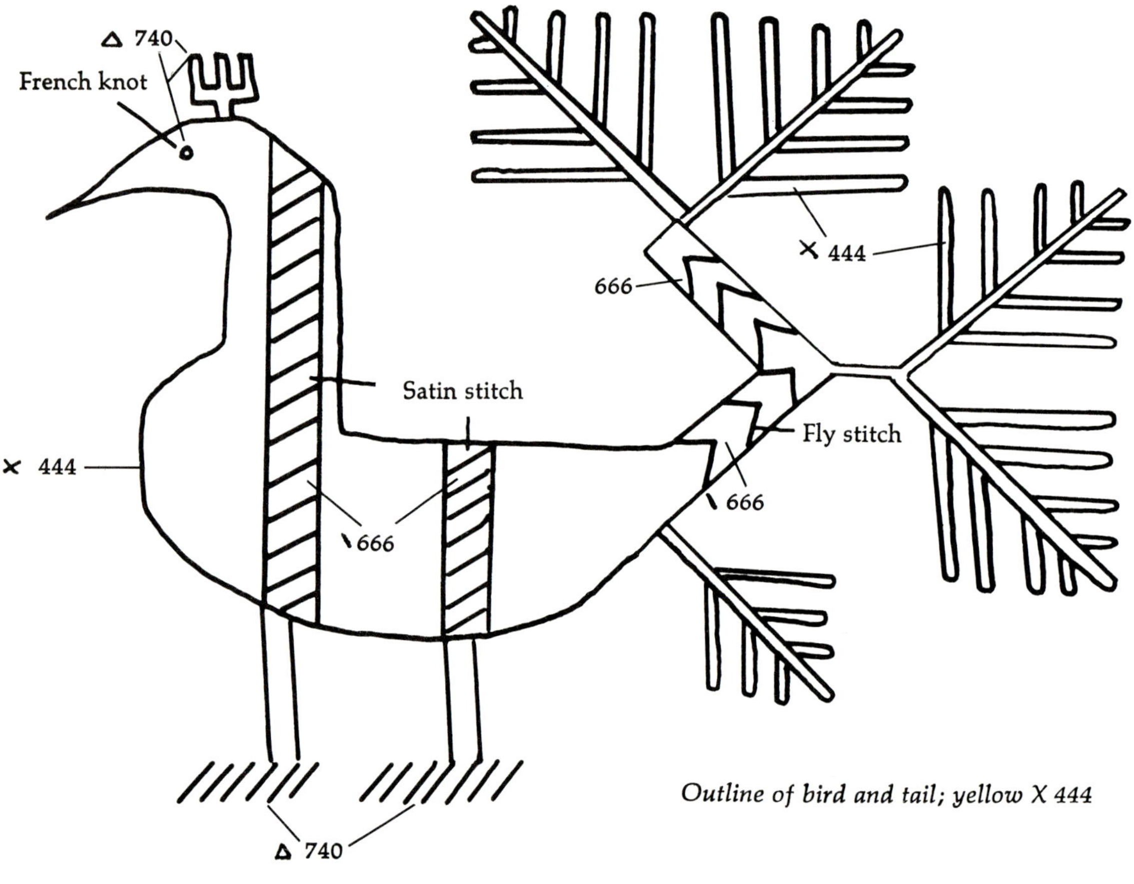

Outline of bird and tail; yellow X 444

The finished size of the bird motif should be 6″ wide from the beak to tail feathers and 5″ high from the top tail feather to the bottom of the foot. To figure out the placement of the birds measure the circumference of the skirt 6″ from the bottom of the finished hem. Mark with a row of basting stitches.

Make a tracing of the bird and place it on the basted line with the bird's feet on the line. Mark the width of the bird with pins and move it a few inches along the line and mark again. You will have to shift the markings a few times until you have the birds evenly placed around the skirt. The size of the space between the birds will depend on the width of the skirt.

Once you have determined the placement of the birds transfer the design all around the skirt. Place on the design, centering it in the hoop, and work the bird, following the diagram for stitch and color placement. Instructions for the stitches can be found on pages 24–29.

PROJECT VI
EMBROIDERED VEST

Inspired by an embroidered Roumanian vest made of sheepskin, this vest is almost completely worked in satin stitch. It is not a small project, but it is simple to do and the time invested will be more than rewarded by the finished product.

What you will need:

Vogue pattern no. 8968 (version B)
Heavyweight linen in the amount called for on the back of the pattern envelope
Fusible interfacing (see pattern)
Lining fabric (see pattern)
Soutache braid
10″ and 5″ embroidery hoops
D.M.C. perlé size 5 (Article 116):
554 Lilac
445 Light yellow
Ecru
D.M.C. six-strand (Article 117):
816 Dark red
905 Green
351 Coral
740 Orange
600 Magenta
369 Light green
320 Green
327 Purple
312 Blue

On the front pattern piece cut off the center to within 1/8″ of the printed center front line. (The vest is made without front fastenings, so the overlap for buttons is not needed. Disregard button and buttonhole markings.)

Cut out the front and back of the vest and the interfacings. Sew the center back seam and press it open. Apply the interfacing to the wrong side of the front and back sections. Sew the front darts and press them open. Stitch around all the edges of the front and back sections 1/8″ from the cut edge. Transfer the design to the front and back over the back seam and front darts, but not along the side back seams. Following the diagram for color placement and stitch direction (indicated by the dotted lines), work the embroidery, using the smaller hoop to reach the embroidery near the edges of the fabric. (See next pages.)

After the embroidery has been completed cut out the lining. Sew the lining to the neckline and armhole seams as indicated in the pattern instructions. Sew the side back seams of the vest and lining as shown in the pattern instructions, but do not bring the lining over the inside of the vest yet. Press the vest seams open and transfer the markings along the side seams. Working with the smaller hoop, finish the embroidery along the seams. Complete the vest according to the pattern directions.

Apply the soutache braid to the front, neckline, and bottom, sewing through the vest fabric and the lining.

The designs used here can be applied to any vest pattern, making adjustments in the spacing of the motif. Use the pattern pieces when placing the designs, remembering to keep the design *within* the cutting lines. In the same way these designs may be used for a simple jacket if the motifs are broken up and spread out.

Note: This vest was made with a medium-yellow-colored linen. The same color combination of threads would be equally effective on a white, off-white, or beige background. It would also be attractive on most dark colors, except green. If you want to use a green fabric, be careful in your choice of the exact shade. Pick one that is darker than the green threads used in the embroidery so that the thread colors will stand out and not get visually "lost."

+	554	Lilac
\	445	Light yellow
•		Ecru
Z	816	Dark red
✱	905	Green
/	351	Coral
I	740	Orange
×	600	Magenta
ǂ	369	Light green
o	320	Green
∽	327	Purple
△	312	Blue

Stitches

1 Satin stitch
2 Back stitch

NOTE: *Except where marked all motifs worked in satin stitch*
Dotted lines indicate direction of stitch

PROJECT VII
WALL HANGING

The design on this hanging is taken from a nineteenth-century Russian towel. Astonishingly, the design has been *simplified* for the hanging. (See pages 87–89 for a little information about Russian towels which are rather special.)

The hanging is rectangular in shape, but by shortening the long sides of the border by removing some of the triangles and placing the bird in the center the design can be made square and used for a cushion.

What you will need:

26″ x 29½″ piece of white or off-white linen
Size 22 crewel or chenille needle
10″ embroidery hoop
Wooden dowels 21½″ or 22″ long
D.M.C. persian (Floralia—Article 484) yarn;

	Ecru
7666	Red
7107	Dark red
7896	Lavender
7245	Purple
7434	Yellow
7344	Green
7742	Orange
7317	Blue

Use one strand of the three-ply yarn.

It is very important that the design be marked on the fabric accurately. The outside of the border should measure 20″ x 23½″. After the border has been marked, center the rooster 5″ from the top line of the bottom border and 4¾″ from the inside line of the left side.

The design is worked in satin stitch and back stitch. Follow the diagram for stitch and color placement. Block the embroidery by soaking it in cold water and lay it right side up on a wooden board that has been covered with an old clean sheet. Tack it down in the four corners with rust-

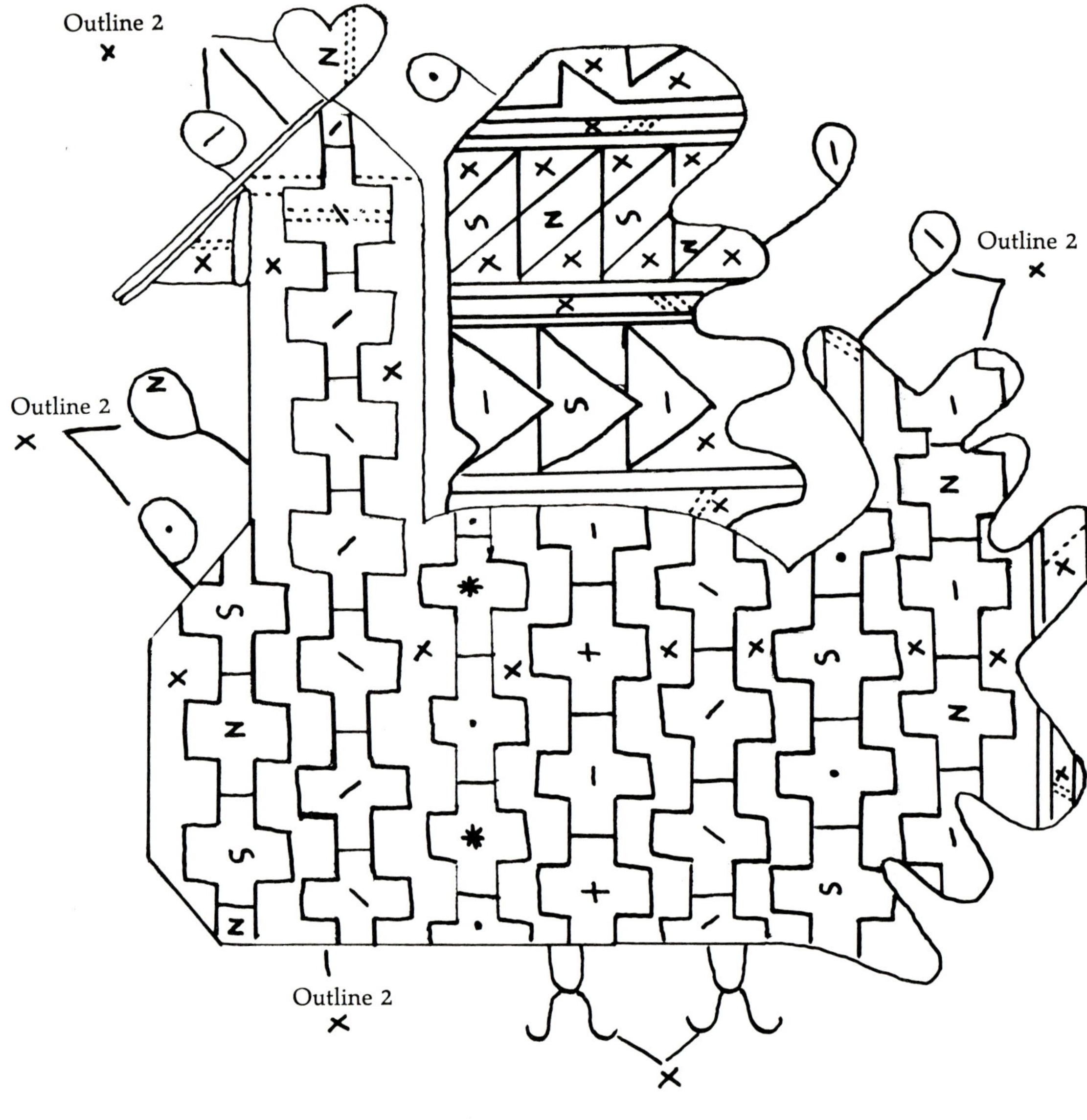

proof tacks. Tack down the sides, top, and bottom every inch or so, being sure that the corners form right angles. Check them with a T square, triangle, or the corner of a book.

When the embroidery is completely dry turn under the fabric on the sides 1/4″. Turn again and sew in place by hand. Turn under 1/4″ on the top and bottom and fold again, leaving an opening large enough to insert the dowels. The ends of the dowels should extend at least 2 inches on each side.

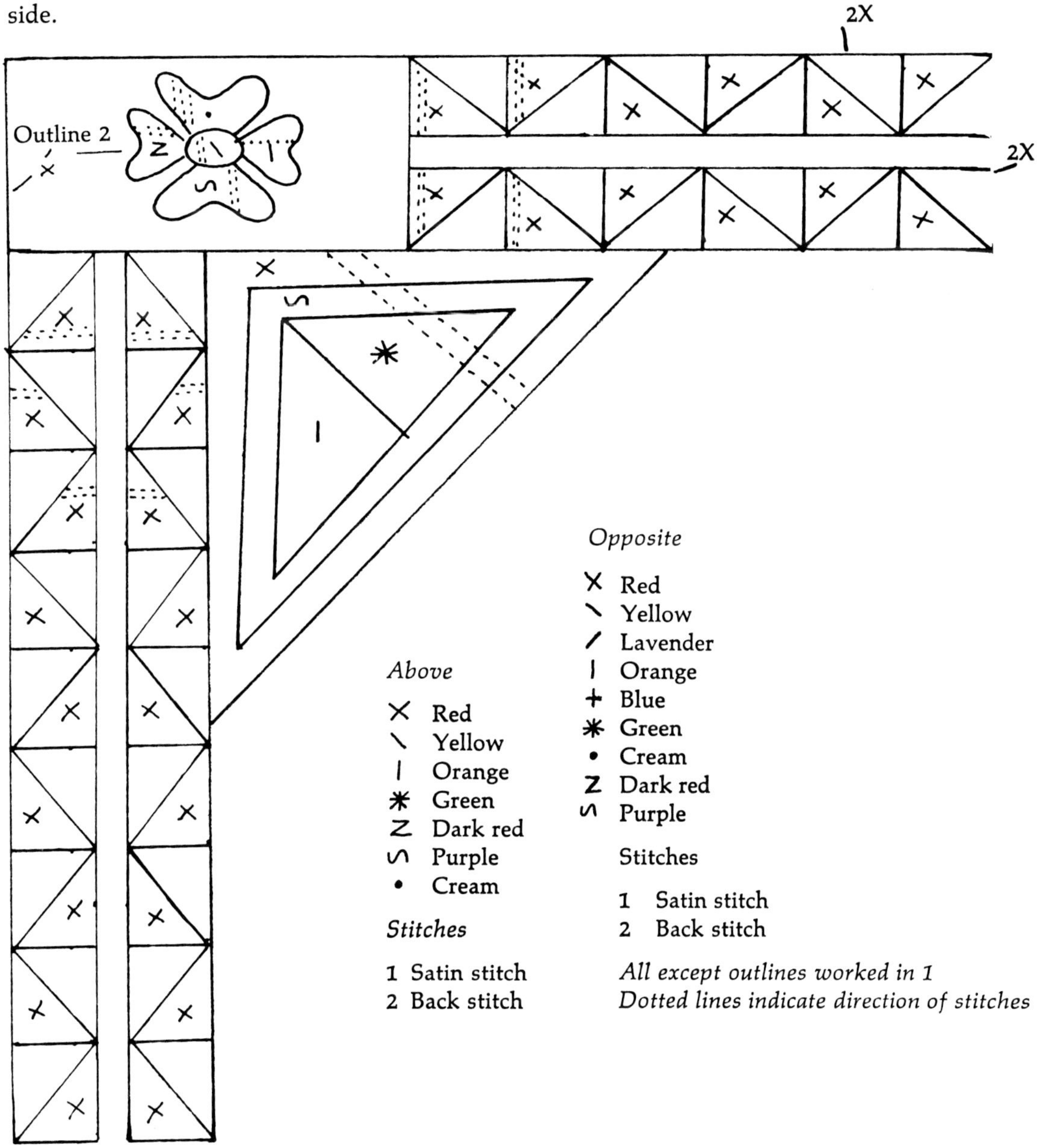

Opposite

- X Red
- \ Yellow
- / Lavender
- | Orange
- + Blue
- ✱ Green
- • Cream
- Z Dark red
- ∽ Purple

Stitches

1 Satin stitch
2 Back stitch

All except outlines worked in 1
Dotted lines indicate direction of stitches

Above

- X Red
- \ Yellow
- | Orange
- ✱ Green
- Z Dark red
- ∽ Purple
- • Cream

Stitches

1 Satin stitch
2 Back stitch

Cross-Stitch Embroidery

PROJECT VIII
TABLE RUNNER

This Russian design can be used on any even-weave fabric for place mats or tablecloths as well as for the runner shown here.

What you will need:

12″ x 44″ Aida cloth 8 blocks to the inch
Size 20 tapestry needle
D.M.C. six-strand (Article 117):
666 Red
797 Blue
Black

× 666 Red
• 797 Blue
Δ Black

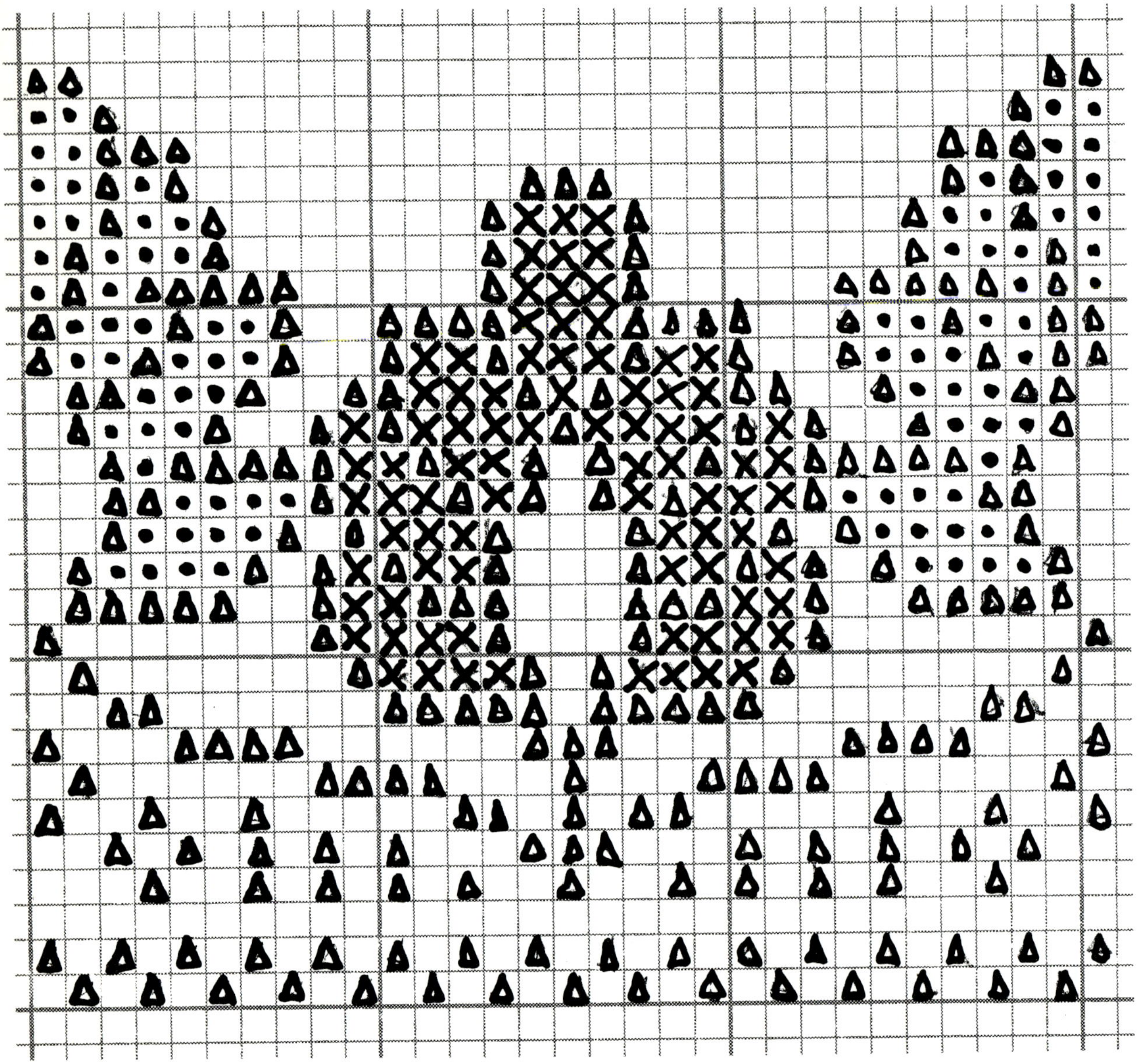

Sew under a ½″ hem on the long sides of the fabric. Start the design on one edge 1″ from the narrow edge. Make a row of black cross stitches the width of the fabric. Start the design following the chart for the placement of the colors. (Note: It is easier if you start with the black first and fill in the colors afterward.)

Finish the other end of the runner with a row of black cross stitches 1″ in from the edge. Carefully remove the vertical threads of the fabric on both ends of the runner to make the fringe.

X 666 Red or
905 Green
Δ Black

PROJECT IX
COASTER MATS

This design of Russian origin can also be used on any even-weave fabric for place mats, napkins, and tablecloths.

What you will need:

One piece of Aida cloth 8 blocks to the inch, 8″ x 8″

D.M.C. six-strand (Article 117):

905 Green or

666 Red

Black

Following the chart, start the design ½″ in from both edges of the fabric. Make the border first. When the design is complete, carefully draw out the cross threads to make the fringe.

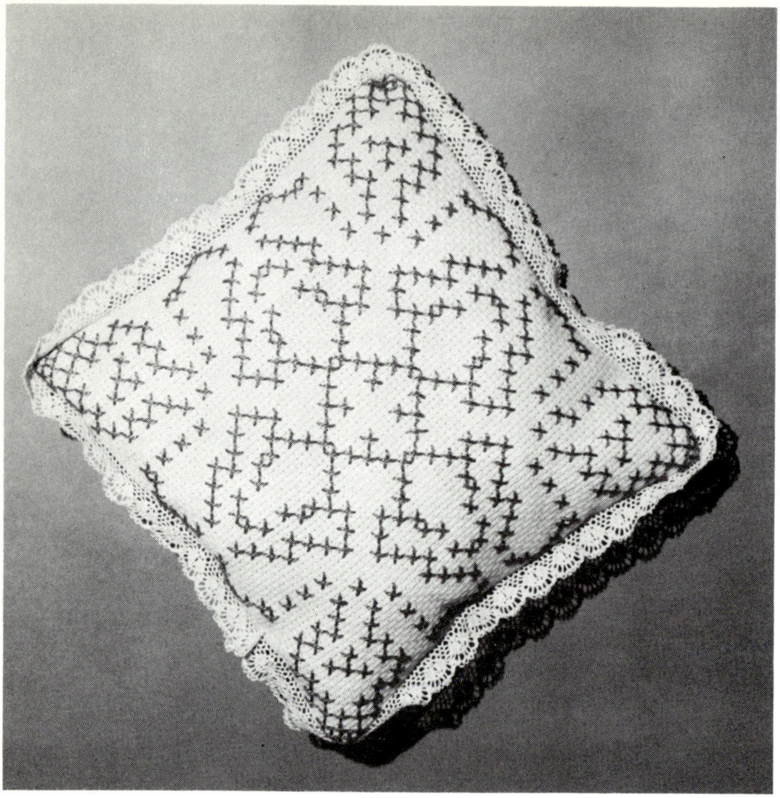

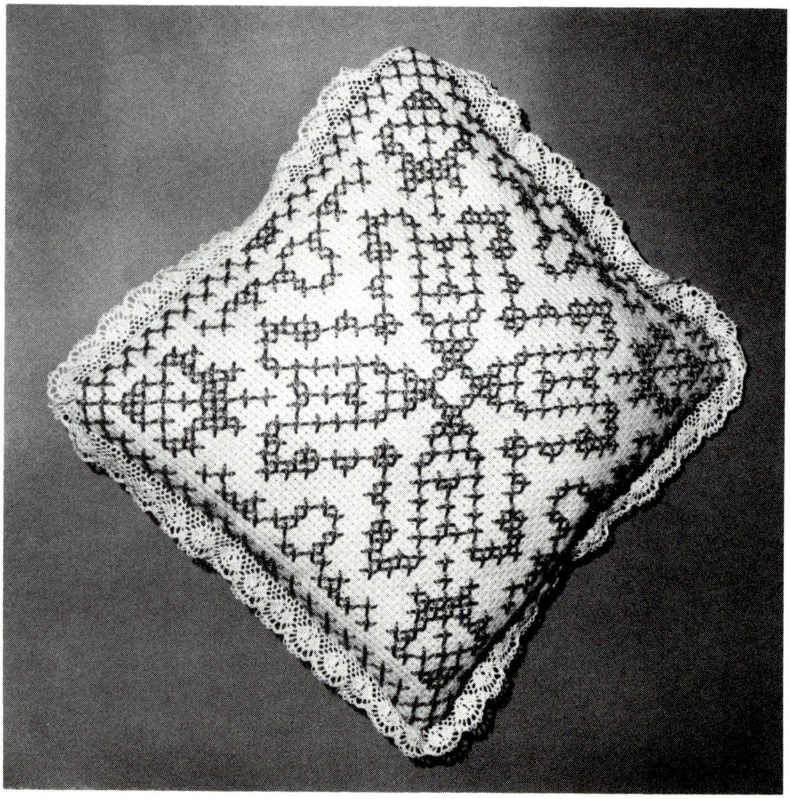

PROJECT X
CROSS-STITCH CUSHIONS

The Russian design on these cushions is made on an 8-block-to-the-inch Aida cloth with each cross stitch covering four blocks vertically and horizontally. The same designs can be worked on any even-weave fabric for place mats, coasters, or the center of a small tablecloth.

For each cushion you will need:

Aida cloth 8 blocks to the inch, one piece 11″ x 11″
Backing fabric the same size
Lace, 1″ wide, 1¼ yards long
Size 20 tapestry needle
Polyester pillow stuffing
D.M.C. perlé size 3 (Article 115):
905 Green or
797 Blue

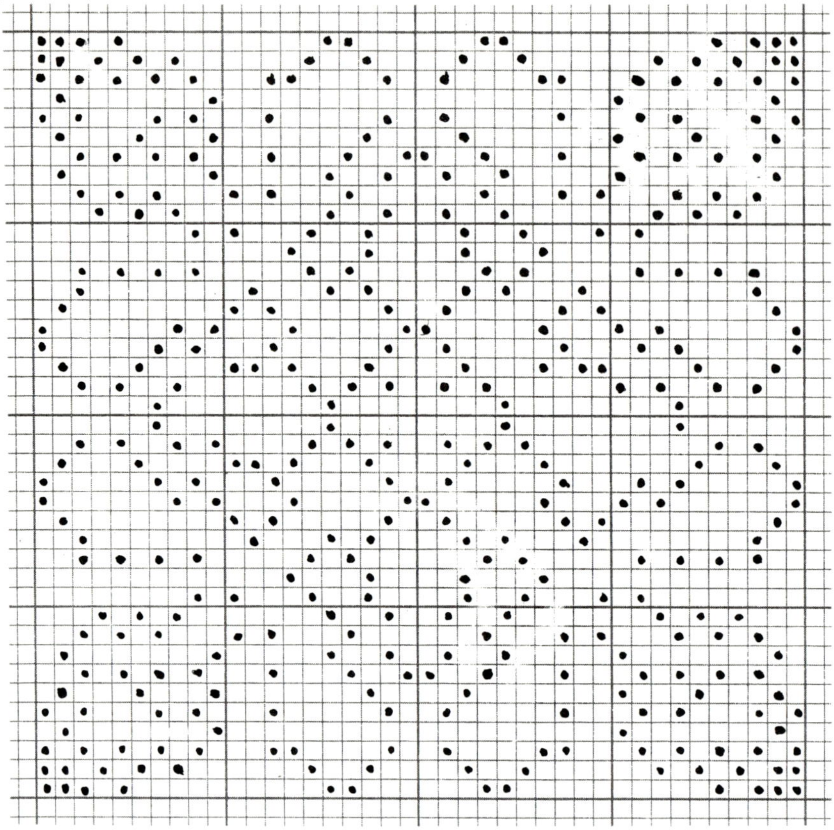

• 905 Green

Start the design at any corner 1″ in from the edges of the fabric and follow the chart.

When the embroidery is finished cut a piece of the backing fabric the same size as the top of the cushion. Cut 40″ of the lace. With the right side of the embroidered cushion top facing you, pin the lace around the edge with the top of the lace facing inward. Sew along the bottom edge

of the lace by hand or machine. Cut off any extra lace. Place the backing on top of the right side of the embroidered top and sew through both layers, keeping the stitching on top of the stitches holding the lace. Be sure not to catch the top of the lace in the stitching. Leave a 5″ opening along one side for turning. Stuff the cushion with polyester filling and sew the opening closed by hand.

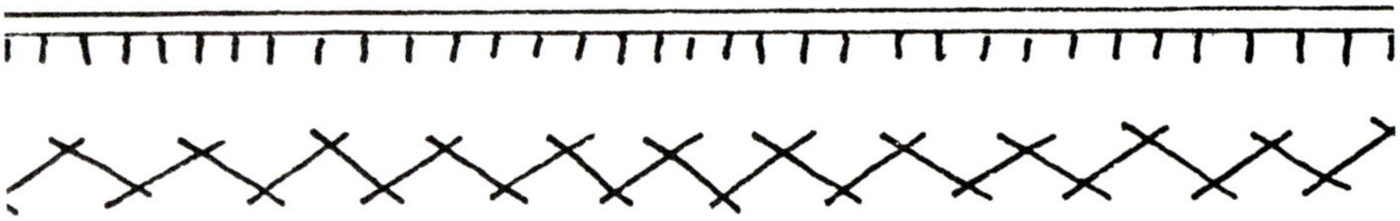

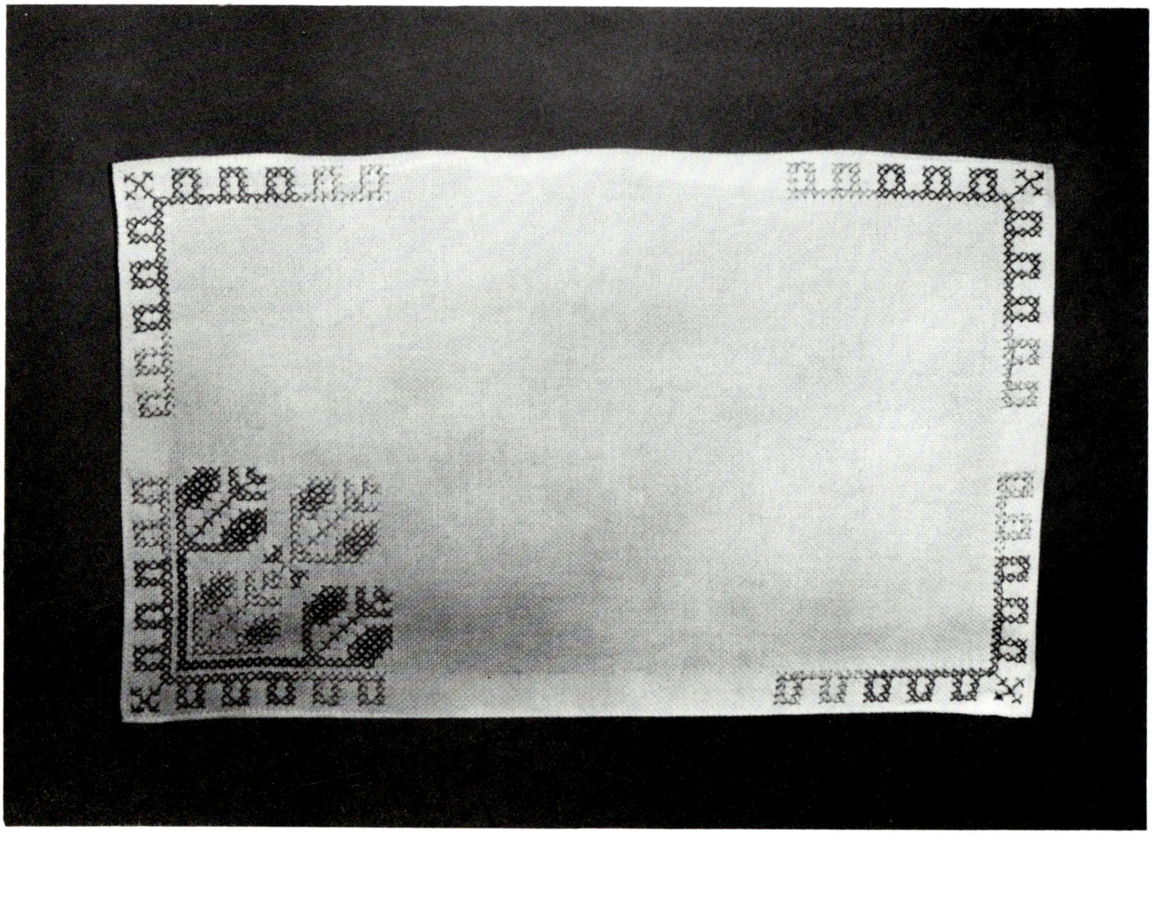

PROJECT XI
PLACE MAT I

This Yugoslavian design looks complex but is delightfully simple to do and works up quickly. The same design can be used for tablecloths and napkins.

What you will need:

Hardanger cloth, one piece 10½″ x 16½″
Size 22 tapestry needle
D.M.C. perlé size 8 (Article 116):
Black
955 Light mint green
740 Orange

or (alternate color combination):
815 Scarlet
827 Light blue
823 Navy

- • 955 Light mint green
- X 740 Orange
- Δ Black

Alternate Color Combination

- • 827 Light blue
- X 815 Scarlet
- Δ 823 Navy

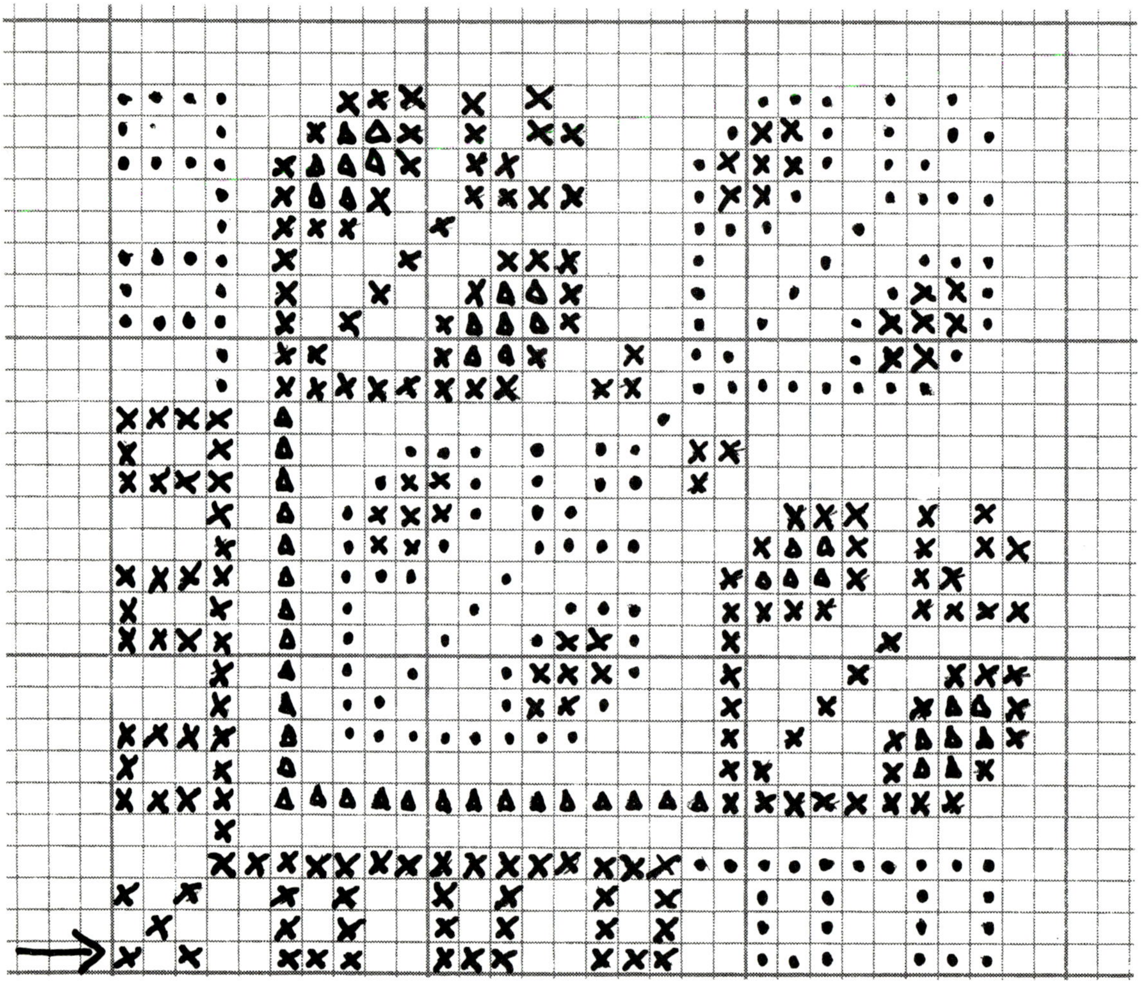

Beginning at the lower left-hand corner 1¼″ from the side and the bottom, start the larger motif with the stitch marked with an arrow on the chart. Follow the chart for the colors and finish the first motif.

Start the other motif at the lower right-hand corner 1¼″ from the right side and along the same row of stitches as the first motif. Begin with the stitch marked with an arrow. Make the same motif in the top right-hand corner 1¼″ from the top, lining up the side with the second motif. Line up the fourth motif with the tip and side threads of the previously worked motifs.

Turn under a hem around the mat so that ½″ extends beyond the embroidery and sew in place by hand or machine.

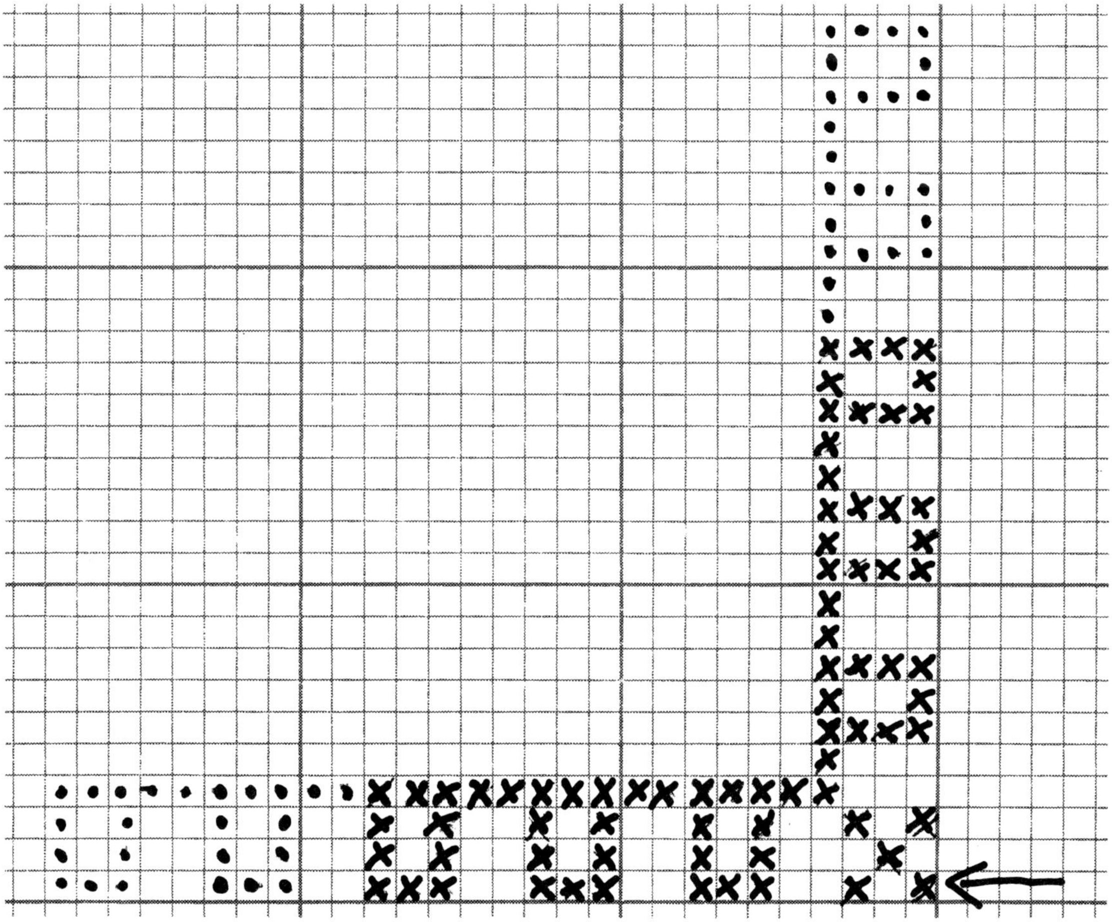

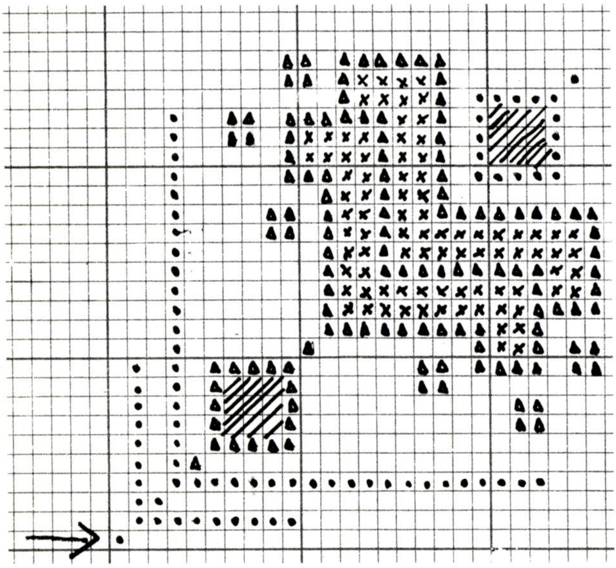

• 955 Green
X 740 Orange (Bosnian stitch)
/ 445 Yellow (satin stitch)
Δ Black

Alternate Color Combination

• 827 Light blue
X 919 Brown red
/ 581 Green
Δ Black

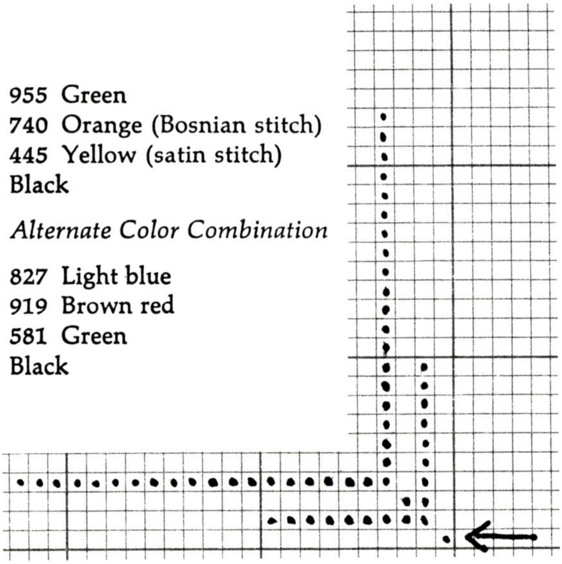

PROJECT XII
PLACE MAT II

This is another Yugoslavian design for a place mat, which requires two other stitches in addition to the regular cross stitch. See the instructions on pages 24 and 26 for working the satin and Bosnian stitches.

What you will need:

Hardanger cloth, one piece 12½″ x 17″
Size 22 tapestry needle

D.M.C. perlé size 8 (Article 116):	or (alternate color combination):
955 Light mint green	919 Brown red
740 Orange	827 Light blue
445 Pale yellow	581 Green
Black	Black

Start at the lower left-hand corner 2″ from the bottom and side of the fabric and make the first stitch marker with an arrow on the chart. Follow the chart for stitch and color placement. Follow the instructions for the place mat on page 73 to finish.

PROJECT XIII
RUSSIAN BLOUSE I

This blouse is made from a pattern out of Hardanger cloth so that the cross stitching can be done directly on the finished garment without using canvas to keep the stitches even. I don't know whether Hardanger cloth has ever been used to make clothes before, but I found it very easy to sew with and the fabric is a perfect weight and finish for this kind of blouse. Because the fabric is 100 percent cotton it is also very pleasant to wear and is completely hand washable.

What you will need:

Vogue pattern no. 9029 or Butterick pattern no. 3997 (blouse version)
White Hardanger cloth in the amount called for on the pattern envelope
Size 22 crewel or chenille needle
D.M.C. six-strand (Article 117):

905 Green
352 Coral

Use three strands of the six-strand floss.

Cut out and make the blouse according to the pattern instructions. Finish completely, including the bottom hem.

Follow the chart to embroider the neckband, neck placket, cuffs, and lower edge of the blouse. Start the embroidery on the lower edge 1¾″ from the bottom of the finished hem. On the front placket space the diamonds between the buttonholes.

PROJECT XIV
RUSSIAN BLOUSE II (ready-made)

The blouse used in this project was purchased and is made of a lightweight crepe that is not an even-weave fabric. The design used here could also be used on the blouse in Project XIII—disregarding reference to canvas.

What you will need:

Ready-made blouse Russian style with the neck placket on the side or in the center

Size 6 crewel or embroidery needle, depending on the weight of the fabric of the blouse. If the blouse is a medium-weight fabric, use a larger needle.

Pieces of 10-mesh mono (single-strand) needlepoint canvas. Note: Do not use interlock canvas.

Sewing thread and needle

D.M.C. six-strand (Article 117):

666 Red
797 Blue

Because the fabric of a purchased blouse is not going to be made of an even-weave fabric it will be necessary to use the needlepoint canvas in order to keep the cross stitches even. Cut the canvas into pieces to fit over the neckband, placket, and cuffs. With the sewing thread baste the canvas to the areas to be embroidered. Following the chart, work the cross stitches over the intersections of the threads of the canvas through all layers of the fabric. When embroidery is finished gently pull the horizontal and vertical threads of the canvas out, using tweezers if necessary.

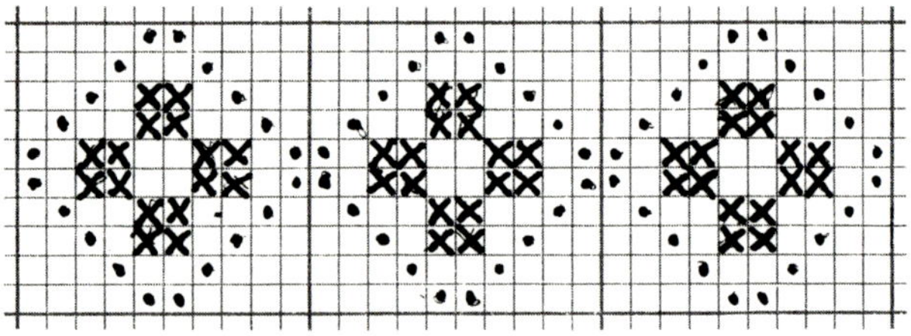

● 905 Green
X 352 Coral

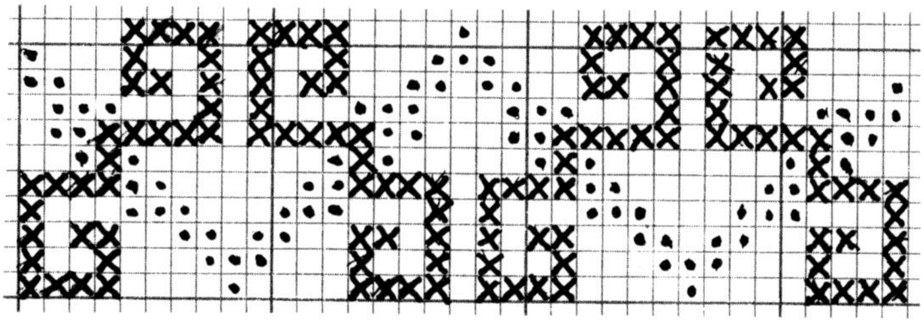

× 666 Red
• 797 Blue

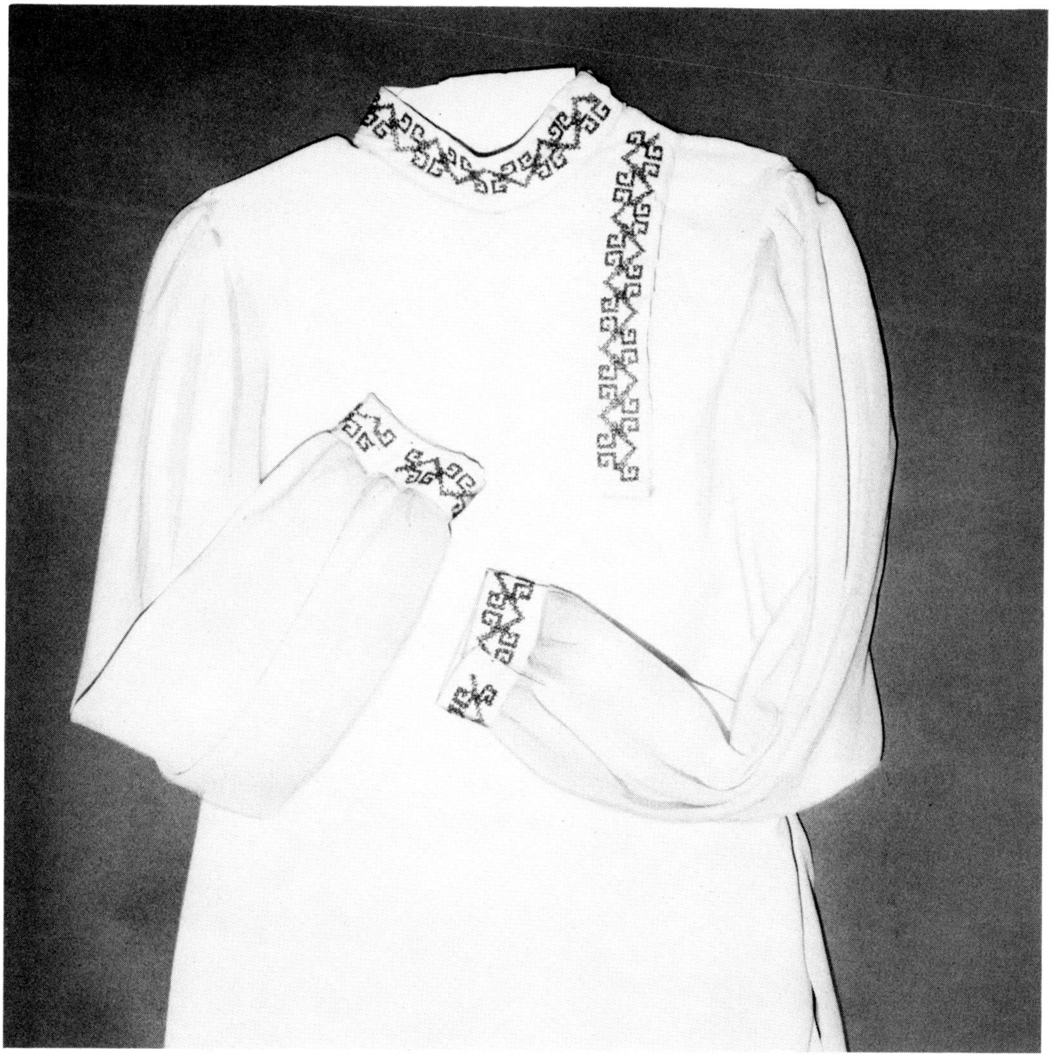

PROJECT XV
TABLECLOTH

This nineteenth-century Russian tablecloth can be a large project as it is, or the design can be used to make a smaller tablecloth, or parts of it can be used for place mats, runners, and napkins.

What you will need:

71″ x 101½″ white linen

Size 6 embroidery or crewel needle

D.M.C. six-strand (Article 117):

899 Pink

2685 Plum

Use three strands of the six-strand floss throughout.

Corner (center and border)

• 899 Pink
X 2685 Plum

Turn under 1/4" around all four sides and press. Turn under a 3/4" hem on all sides, press, and sew in place by hand or machine. Fold the fabric in half and in half again to determine the center. Mark the center with rows of basting stitches. Start the corner of the center approximately 20" (measured diagonally) from the center. Follow the chart for color and stitch placement. Work the border starting with a corner and follow the photograph for the placement of the leaf motifs. Work the scattered leaf motifs halfway between the bottom of the center embroidery and the top of the border.

Border and scattered motif

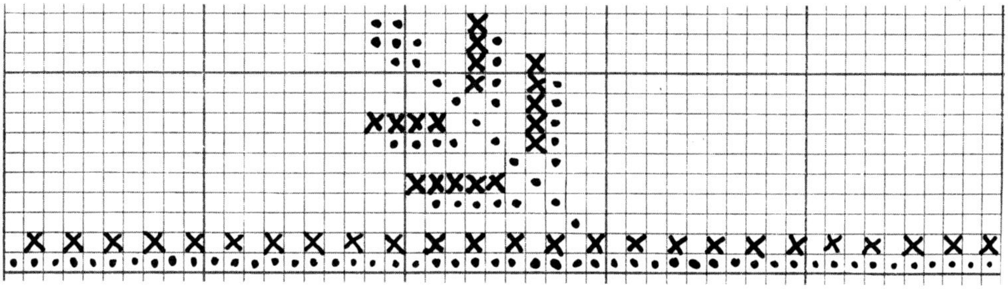

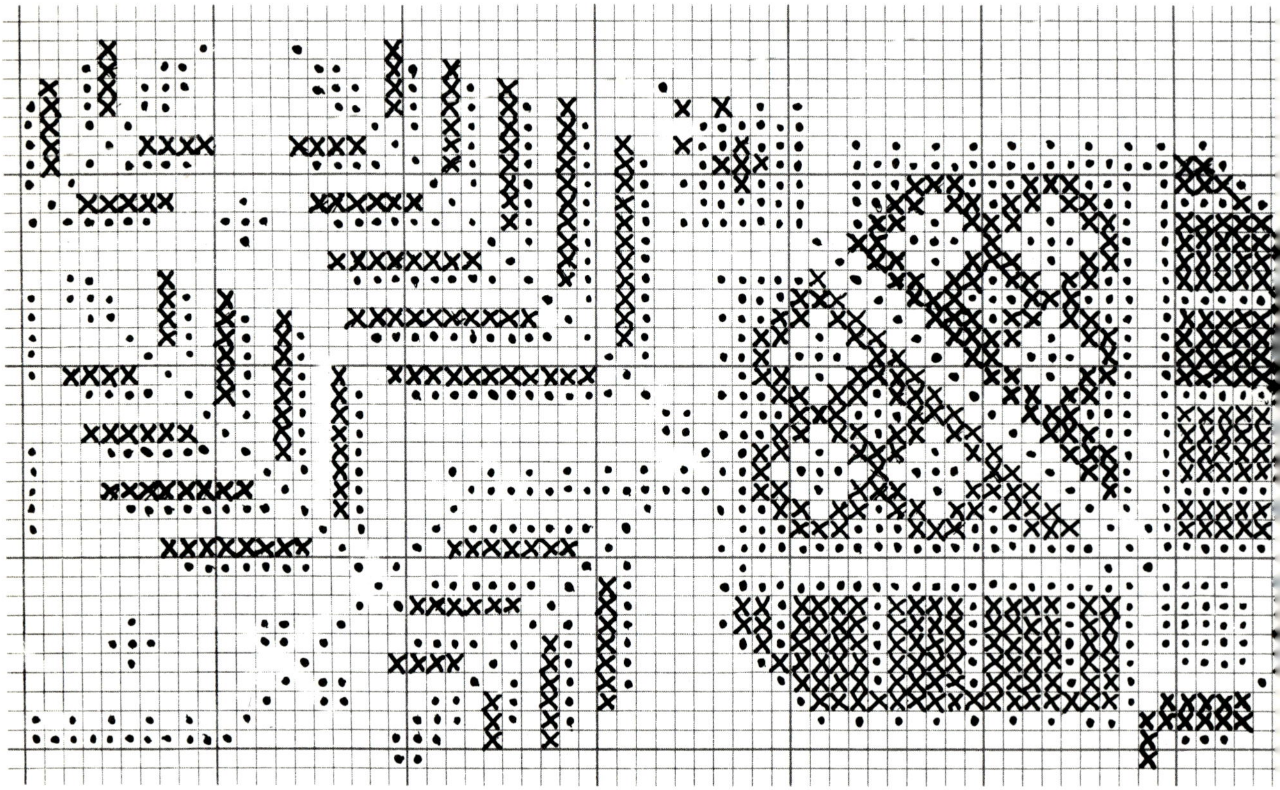

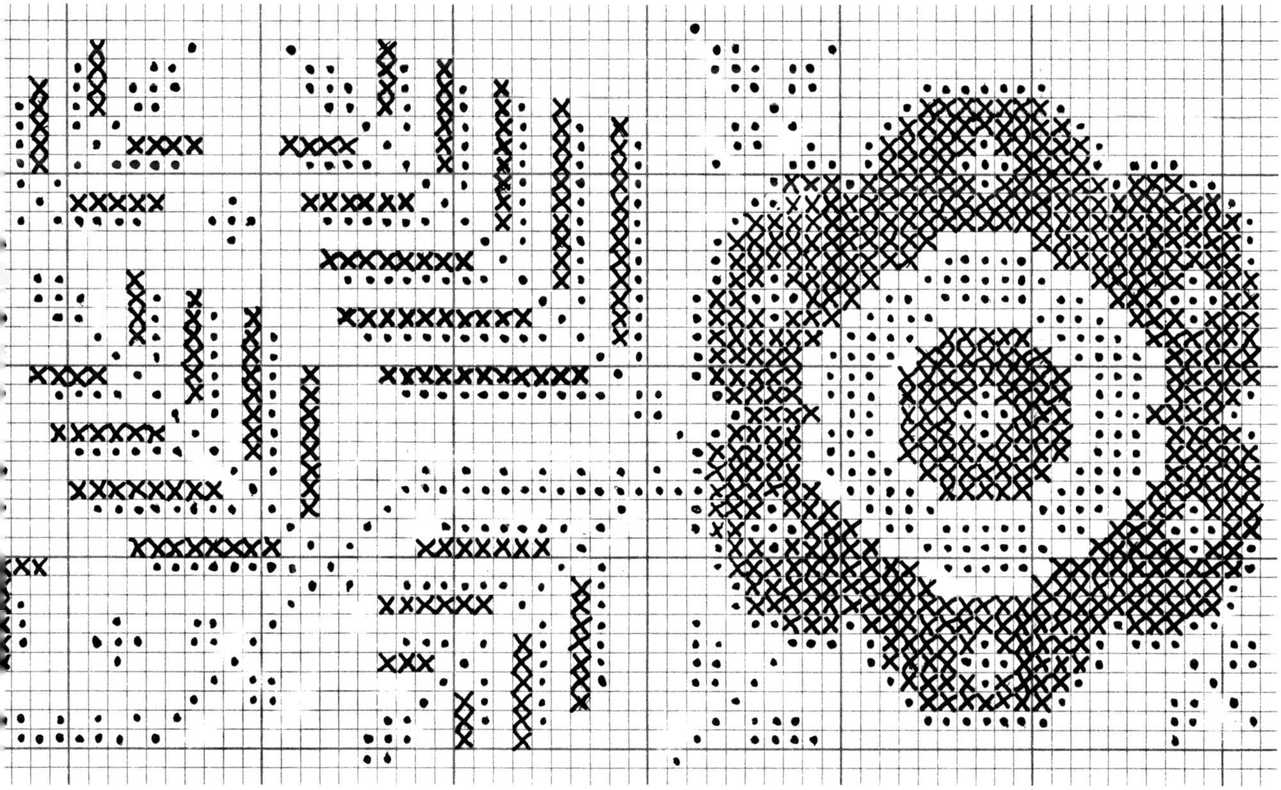
Center repeat
• 899 Pink
X 2685 Plum

Russian towel (around 1900). COURTESY OLGA LEY.

The Russian Towel

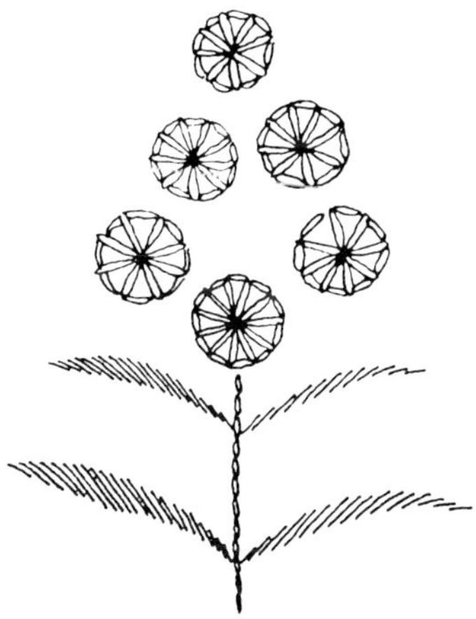

The traditional Russian towels are unlike anything to be found in a Western linen closet. They are made of linen and usually measure about 14″ wide and are over 7′ long. The usual story told by a Russian when asked why the towels were so long is that they were used by the men who would sit around all day drinking glass after glass of very hot tea. The tea was so hot that one end of the towel was placed under the glass to protect the top of the table and the other end was used to mop the brow of the overheated tea drinker.

Actually they were used for a large variety of household purposes, from dusting to hand wiping. They were always embroidered and many of them have more elaborate embroidered designs than we would expect to find on a simple piece of utilitarian linen.

The simple cross-stitch design on one nineteenth-century towel inspired the design used for the blouse in Project XIII. A much more elaborate towel now in the State Historical Museum in Moscow provided the design of the wall hanging in Project VII.

Reproducing these towels as they were would be very difficult today, as the fabric for them was woven on looms that were just as wide as the finished towel, thus eliminating the need for side hems. If used, these hems would be bulky and would not capture the feeling of the originals. Also, it would be difficult to adapt the extremely long towels to our way of life. They belong to another country and other times.

Russian towel (around 1900). COURTESY OLGA LEY.

The importance of these unusual pieces of household linen lies in the embroidered designs on them, which can be the sources of inspiration for decorating many of our own linens and clothes.

In this section there are pictures of some of these Russian towels as well as other Slavic linens and garments whose embroidery can serve to fire your imagination to create your own projects using these designs.

If you are interested in finding even more sources of Slavic designs, see the bibliography at the end of this book. The Slavonic departments of large libraries and the textile departments of museums can supply an almost never-ending source of beautiful designs.

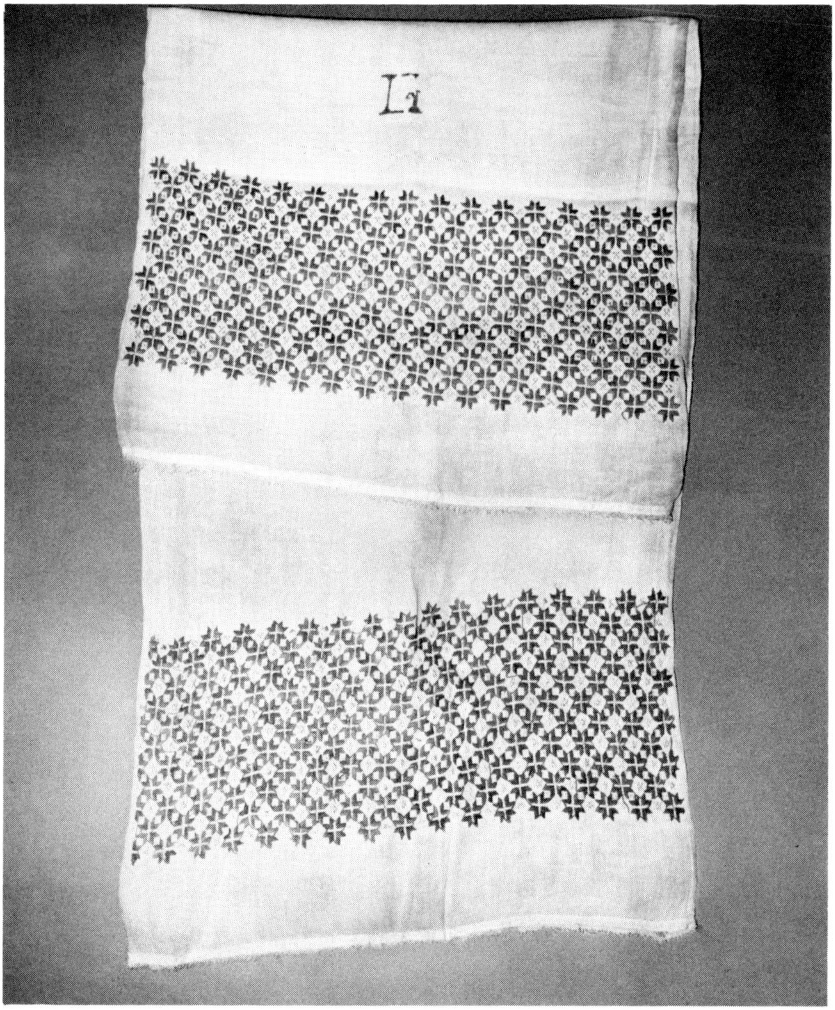

Russian towel (late nineteenth century). COURTESY LUCY KORTCHMAR.

Above, Present-day Yugoslavian blouse with cross-stitch embroidery.
COURTESY VICTORIA POWER.

Opposite, Tenth-century Russian folk apron with counted-stitch embroidery.
COURTESY LUCY KORTCHMAR.

Nineteenth-Century Russian coaster mats, embroidered by nuns at a convent at which embroidery commissions were taken. COURTESY LUCY KORTCHMAR.

SUPPLIERS

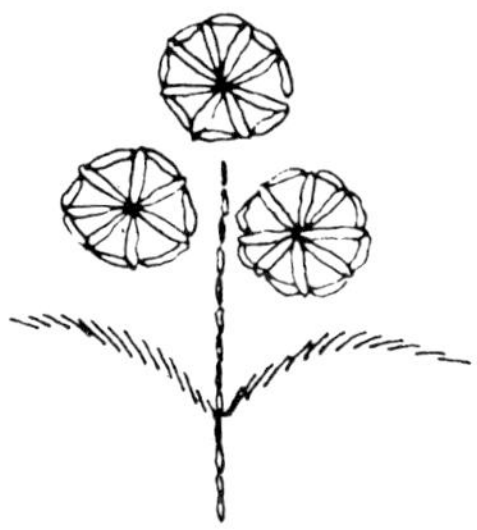

D.M.C. yarns, threads, and Aida cloth and Hardanger cloth can be ordered by mail from the following stores if they are not available in your area. These stores will send catalogs:

Herrschners
Stevens Point
Wisconsin 54481

Merribee
2904 West Lancaster
P.O. Box 9680
Fort Worth, Texas 76107

LeeWards
1200 St. Charles Road
Elgin, Illinois 60120

If you still have difficulty in obtaining the materials you need, write directly to the addresses below for the name of your local distributor:

The D.M.C. Corporation
107 Trumbull Street
Elizabeth, New Jersey 07206

or, in Canada:

Belding-Corticelli, Ltd.
P.O. Box 9
Montreal 101, Canada

In England:
To obtain the names of stores that carry D.M.C. thread and yarn:
C & F Handicraft Supplies Ltd.
346 Stag Lane
Kingsbury, London N.W.9

For Aida and Hardanger cloth and other embroidery supplies:
The Needlewoman
146 Regent Street
London W.1

BIBLIOGRAPHY

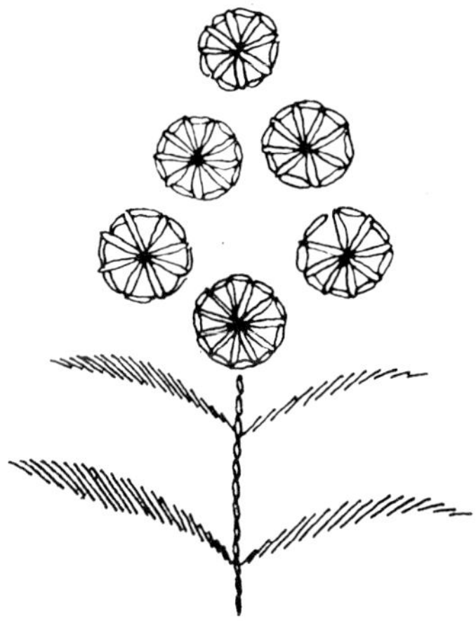

Gillon, Edmund V., Jr. *Geometric Design and Ornament.* New York: Dover Publications, 1969.

Wilson, Erica. *Erica Wilson's Embroidery Book.* New York: Charles Scribner's Sons, 1973.

The D.M.C. Library:

Czechoslovakian Embroideries
Yugoslavian Embroideries, First Series
Yugoslavian Embroideries, Second Series
Bulgarian Embroideries